Opiate Addiction - The Painkiller Addiction Epidemic, Heroin Addiction and the Way Out

by Taite Adams

Rapid   Response   Press
1730 Lighthouse Terr S., Suite 12

St.   Petersburg,   FL   33707
www.rapidresponsepress.com

Ordering   Information:
Quantity sales. Special discounts are available on quantity purchases by corporations, associations, and others. For details, contact the publisher   at   the   address   above.
Orders by U.S. trade bookstores and wholesalers. Please contact Rapid Response Press: Tel: (866) 983-3025; Fax: (855) 877-4736 or visit www. rapidresponsepress.com.

Printed in the United States of America

Publisher's   Cataloging-in-Publication   data
Adams,   Taite.
A title of a book : a subtitle of the same book / Taite Adams.
p.   cm.
ISBN   978-0-9889875-5-5
1. The main category of the book —Health —Other category. 2. Another subject category —Mind and Body. 3. More categories — Recovery.

Fourth Edition

==================

Limit of Liability/Disclaimer of Warranty

===============

Disclaimer

===============

Medical Disclaimer

The information contained in this book is not intended to serve as a replacement for professional medical advice. Any use of the information in this book is at the reader's discretion. The author and publisher specifically disclaim any and all liability arising directly or indirectly from the use or application of any information contained in this book. A health care professional should be consulted regarding your specific situation.

To my Son - You have always been my light; without you, it could have been very bleak indeed;

To Mom - Your example of perseverance hasn't gone unnoticed;

To my Love - Your enthusiasm for all that life offers makes me love and cherish you more and more each day. You continue to inspire me beyond words.

Get All The Books In The Series:

Kickstart Your Recovery - The Road Less Traveled to Freedom From Addiction

Safely Detox From Alcohol and Drugs at Home

Restart Your Recovery - 12 Things You Can Do To Get Back on the Beam

Who is Molly?: Molly Drug Facts, What is Ecstasy, and Life-Saving MDMA Effects Info

E-Go: Ego Distancing Through Mindfulness, Emotional Intelligence, and the Language of Love

Beyond Benzos - Benzo Addiction, Benzo Withdrawal, and Long-term Recovery from Benzodiazepines

Senior Addiction - Drug Addiction in Older Adults, Senior Alcoholism, and Recovery Solutions

Boundaries in Recovery: Emotional Sobriety Through Setting Personal Limitations

See http://www.TaiteAdams.com for more info

Table of Contents

Preface

The world of opiate addiction is ever-changing and has a lot to do with market conditions. Supply and demand and basic economics play a greater role than many people realize in which drugs come in and out of fashion at a particular point in time. Regardless of which form of opiates are popular at the present moment, there is little doubt that opiates will always be one of the most widely abused classes of drugs. Whether it be Vicodin, Oxys, Perc 30s, methadone or heroin, the opiate addict will generally take what they can get their hands on and then abuse the hell out of it. And, unfortunately, the results are often deadly. There are over 43,000 drug overdose deaths per year in the United States, 70 percent of which are opioid-related.

Opiates have a very long and rich history of being "in fashion", later shunned by society and then finding their medicinal use for the management of pain. It was this rise in the use of prescription opiate painkillers, however, that has brought about what the CDC is now calling an epidemic of prescription drug addiction. In fact, in 2014 nearly 1.9 million Americans were addicted to some form of prescription painkiller, more than those addicted to cocaine and heroin combined. I had already been clean from my opiate addiction for over 13 years by this time, yet the memory of the day to day struggle, the terror and hopelessness, are still fresh in my mind. This is not something that I expect to ever forget and it was interesting to re-live some of it and learn a few new "tricks" in the writing of this book.

What scares the hell out of me more than anything else is the rising problem, in epidemic proportions, of heroin use in this country as a direct result of prescription opiate addiction. There is no doubt that prescription painkillers serve as a gateway to heroin use and this is deadly. While abuse of prescription pills for pain was reported to be going down in 2011, according to the national survey on drug use and health, heroin use was reported to be increasing. In fact, in 2011, nearly 200,000 people tried heroin for the first time. By 2014, the rates for prescription drug abuse were back up into the stratosphere and heroin abuse nearly out of control, with an estimate of over 700,000 Americans having used the drug.

If you or a loved one are addicted to opiates, this book is for you. In it you can learn more about the drugs that you have been taking, their effects on your body and mind, and what you can do to break free. There is information on opiate maintenance programs as well as warnings on their long-term use and some good information about opiate detox and making treatment center decisions. Recovery from opiate addiction isn't easy but it is absolutely possible and I have found that it is infinitely simpler and more fulfilling than that of the day to day life of a hopeless opiate addict.

The Opiate Addiction Epidemic

Nobody will laugh long who deals much with opium: its pleasures even are of a grave and solemn complexion. -Thomas de Quincey

Most people think that they have a clear picture in their mind of what a drug addict is but generally, when it comes to opiate addiction, what you get couldn't be further from that image. Opiate addicts do not fit a general stereotype as the drug does not discriminate. Because of the nature of opiate addiction, it strikes across age, ethnic and economic groups and then pulls each and every one of those stricken down with equal measure.

The CDC recently reported that opiate addiction is now America's fastest-growing drug problem, with the total number of painkillers prescribed in a single year enough to medicate every adult living in the U.S. around the clock. While true that heroin is the most widely used illegal opiate, it's a fact that prescription opiate painkillers are equally dangerous and an insidious problem. The World Health Organization (WHO) estimates that approximately two million people in the United States alone are addicted to prescription opiates.

The problem is also not limited to adults, as first use of opiates seems to be getting younger. The National Institute on Drug Abuse (NIDA) reports that an estimated 52 million people, 20% of those aged 12 and older, have used prescription drugs for nonmedical reasons at least once. Also, about 1 in 12 high school seniors reported nonmedical use of the prescription drug Vicodin during the past year. About 1 in 20 high school seniors also reported abusing OxyContin. This isn't limited to the younger crowd either. According to a 2011 study by the Substance Abuse and Mental Health Services Administration

(SAMHSA), the rate of current illicit drug use in adults aged 50 to 59 increased to 6.3% in 2011 from 2.7% in 2002 with opiates being among the most commonly abused drugs. The total number of opiate prescriptions dispensed by retail pharmacies in the United States rose from 76 million in 1991 to 217 million in 2012.

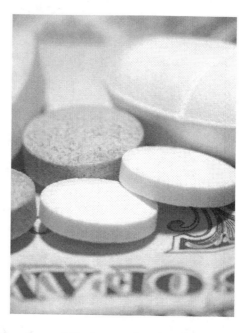

The epidemic of opiate addiction and painkiller addiction has resulted in nearly 30,000 overdose deaths annually. While heroin continues to be a rising problem, opiate addiction, in general, is not the stereotypical drug problem that many of us think of when we picture the "war on drugs." In fact, many times this involves a patient who began with a legitimate pain issue, an unwitting string of physicians (or not) who are writing these prescriptions, and pharmaceutical companies who are (debatably) acting within the law. The public consumption of opiates, through legal channels, is costing health insurers over $72 billion annually.

Opiates are a huge problem! ...and growing. Trust me, I know. Most of the time we start taking them for a legitimate pain issue, whether for a root canal or some major surgery. Many times the addiction to them develops over a period of time as a physical dependency develops.

With others, however, there is an instantaneous "pull" that these drugs have on you because of the way that they make you feel. They not only take away the physical pain that they were prescribed for but bring to the table something that you thought you had been looking for for a very long time. This is how it was for me. Those pills became my best friend and my salvation for a time - until they completely owned me.

You will find peace not by trying to escape your problems, but by confronting them courageously. You will find peace not in denial, but in victory. -J. Donald Walters

Definition of Opiates and History

Opium teaches only one thing, which is that aside from physical suffering, there is nothing real. -Andre Malraux

Opiates, by definition, are considered to be the natural alkaloids found in the resin of the opium poppy (Papaver somniferum). However, some definitions of opiates include the semi-synthetic substances that are directly derived from the opium poppy as well. As such, opiates themselves can be natural or synthetic. Natural opiates include opium, morphine, and codeine. Other substances that are man-made are called opioids. These are most used to treat chronic pain and are also highly addictive. These include Vicodin, Oxycodone, Demerol, and Dilaudid. Heroin is actually an opioid manufactured from morphine.

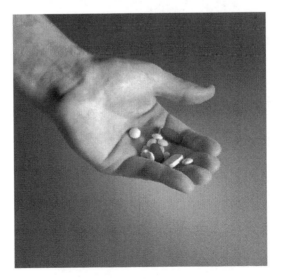

While opiate addiction is at the forefront of the news and wreaking havoc in so many lives in the present day, it is by no means a new phenomenon. In fact, the first opiates were believed to have been cultivated and used during the Neolithic period (the new stone age). The Sumerian, Egyptian, Greek, Roman, Persian and Arab Empires all used opiates as a potent pain relief measure, even allowing for prolonged surgical procedures. The first written reference to the poppy used to produce opium appears in a Sumerian text dated around 4,000 B.C. Homer speaks of its' effects in The Odyssey. Telemachus is depressed after failing to find his father, Odysseus. But then Helen...

"...had a happy thought. Into the bowl in which their wine was mixed, she slipped a drug that had the power of robbing grief and anger of their sting and banishing all painful memories. No one who swallowed this dissolved in their wine could shed a single tear that day, even for the death of his mother or father, or if they put his brother or his own son to the sword and he were there to see it done..."

Images of poppies appear in Egyptian pictography and Roman sculptures. Also, representations of the Greek and Roman gods of sleep, Hypnos and Somnos, often show them wearing or carrying poppies. Opium was readily bought on the streets of Rome. Opium use had spread to India, China, and Arabia by the eighth century A.D. Arabs both used opium and organized its trade.

In China, recreational use of the drug began in the 15th century and increased to near epidemic levels until the 17th century, when opium prohibition began there. This followed another two centuries of increased opium use and several trade "opium-related" wars. By 1905, nearly 25% of the male population of China were regular opium users.

Opium is said to have been used for recreational purposes from the 14th century onward. Philippus Aureolus Theophrastus Bombastus von Hohenheim (1490-1541), better known as Paracelsus, claimed: "I possess a secret remedy which I call *laudanum* and which is superior to all other heroic remedies". He concocted laudanum [literally: "something to be praised"] by extracting opium into brandy, thus producing, in effect, tincture of morphine.

British opium imports rose from a brisk 91,000 lbs in 1830 to an astonishing 280,000 lbs in 1860. The mid-nineteenth century invention of the hypodermic syringe and the use of injectable morphine as a pain reliever during the American Civil War led to the first wave of morphine addiction. The most important reason for the increase in opiate consumption in the United States during the 19th century was the prescribing and dispensing of legal opiates by physicians and pharmacists to women with "female problems" (mostly to relieve menstrual pain). Between 150,000 and 200,000 opiate addicts lived in the United States in the late 19th century and between two-thirds and three-quarters of these addicts were women

In 1895, Heinrich Dreser, working for the Bayer Company in Germany, synthesized heroin. Bayer began to market the drug in 1898. In the early 1900s, heroin was seen as a potential solution to the increasing problem of morphine addiction, and the philanthropic St. James Society mounted a campaign to mail free samples of heroin to morphine addicts. Heroin addiction grew, particularly in northern industrial slums.

There were no legal restrictions on the use or importation of opium in the U.S. until the San Francisco Opium Den Ordinance of 1875, which banned the public smoking of opium. Global regulation of opium began in the early 20th century, with the formation of the International Opium Commission in 1909. During this same year, importation of opium into the United States was banned altogether under the Opium Exclusion Act. By 1914, 34 nations had agreed that the production and importation of opiates should be controlled or reduced. Subsequently, the League of Nations took over and all participating nations agreed to prohibit the import, sale, distribution, and export of narcotic drugs except for medicinal and scientific purposes.

This certainly wasn't the end of the opium epidemic, as we well know. In fact, heroin had its second wave of popularity in the United States in the 1930's and 1940's in the Harlem Jazz Scene and again in the Beatnik subculture of the 1950's. There was also the issue of widespread abuse amongst U.S. servicemen in Vietnam, pushing the issue to the forefront of Nixon's drug policy agenda.

Vast improvements in the purity of street heroin in the 1980's and 1990's created the potential for the drug to be snorted and smoked. Subsequently, heroin usage increased significantly in the 1990's. Historically, a majority of the drug came to the U.S. through the French Connection of the Golden Triangle of Southeast Asia (Burma, Thailand, Laos), however, recent years have shown the South American drug organizations to be expanding their cocaine markets into the heroin market as well.

Heroin itself went out of favor for a time, but its popularity has seen a resurgence in the past few years due to several factors that are discussed a bit later. The use and abuse of prescription opiates have been declared an "epidemic" by this country's CDC and drug companies continue to scramble in an effort to produce formulations of their drugs that are not susceptible to diversion and abuse. Opiates are a powerful draw, however, and addicts are incredibly cunning and resilient when it comes to finding ways to use and abuse them.

Clearly opiates have a long history of use, both medicinally and recreationally. The historical problem is the same one that exists today. These drugs have pain relief properties that serve a very real and valuable purpose for many people. However, due to their specific action on the brain (which we are about to get into), they are highly addictive and very susceptible to abuse. Ongoing controversies abound as to their continued use for chronic pain, the cost of opiate addiction, opiate maintenance therapy and even opiate detox procedures. Each one of these issues will be discussed in coming chapters.

How Opiates Work

*Whether you sniff it smoke it eat it or shove it
up your ass the result is the same: addiction. -
William S. Burroughs*

Describing addiction itself is a tall order, and opiate addiction is so prolific that it has been studied at length. However, the best place to start is perhaps by understanding just how opiates work and the effect that they have on our bodies and our brain. Natural opiates are derived from the dried "mild" of the opium poppy while synthetic opiates are manufactured in chemical laboratories with a similar chemical structure. Regardless, the effect on the body and brain is essentially the same.

Opiates work in the central nervous system (CNS) as a CNS depressant. They slow breathing, heart rate and brain activity in the user. Opiates can also cause a reduction in sexual drive, a suppressed appetite and increased muscle tension. Opiates have a tendency to induce euphoria by affecting the brain regions that control pleasure. Users report feeling warm, sleepy and content. Opiates also can cause constipation, widening of the blood vessels and depress coughing and breathing reflexes.

Opiates resemble natural chemicals that bind to neurotransmitters in the brain called opiate receptors. There are three types of opiate receptors in the brain, and each has a different function. Pain relief, pleasure and feelings of well-being and euphoria are controlled by these receptors. The opiate receptors are predominantly, but not exclusively, located in what is called the limbic system. The opiate receptor that is thought to be associated with the intense pleasure of opiate use is termed the mu receptor, and it is the receptor stimulated by heroin and morphine. Additionally, opiates affect many other locations in the brain and CNS, including:

- Limbic System- controls emotions, feelings of pleasure, relaxation and contentment

- Brain Stem- controls the autonomic nervous system functions like breathing and heart rate

- Spinal Cord- controls sensations in the body like responses to pain even in the case of serious injury

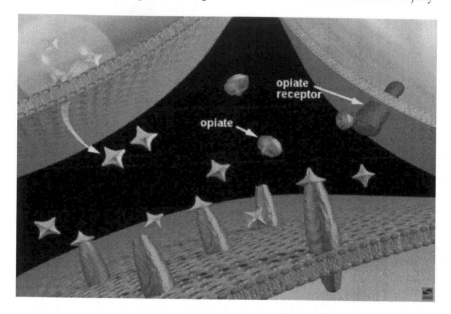

According to the National Institute on Drug Abuse (NIDA), the method in which opiates are used plays a key role in how quickly they are absorbed by the body, and consequently their effects. The weight of the user and the amount of the drug consumed also play a role. The way in which the drugs are used often depends on the particular drug. Many opiates can be swallowed as pills. Others can be injected, snorted or even smoked. Some prescription opiates are taken with alcohol or other drugs to intensify the effect.

One of the most important things to note here was mentioned just a moment ago. This is that opiates "resemble natural chemicals" that bind to neurotransmitters in the brain. What this means is that the body is already capable of producing these "feel good" chemicals in the brain to bind to its opiate receptors. Our brains are naturally capable of calling forth feelings of pleasure, contentment, relaxation and even pain relief. However, once we start putting something unnatural into the mix and bombarding our system with synthetic happiness, the body and brain forget that it's capable of doing this on its own and becomes dependent upon the unnatural solution. A solution that, in time, is going to stop working anyway.

Opiate addiction is characterized by a marked increase in tolerance for the drug used and, should the user also have pain issues, a recurrence of the original underlying symptoms. This is an absolutely maddening cycle. I know because I lived it. I began taking Vicodin in my early twenties for some moderate neck pain. I became immediately addicted because I loved the pills and the feeling they gave me. What I found, though, was that I needed to take more and more of them to get the desired effect. So much so that, in the end, I was taking over 30 pills a day and I could have taken a lot more had I had access to them. Through most of this, I wasn't taking the pills for fun anymore. That was only in the very beginning when I was being enticed and romanced by the drug. No, I was only taking them to feel "normal" and avoid getting sick. This is a horrific way to live but painkiller addiction is powerful.

Drugs are a bet with your mind.   - Jim Morrison

Unfortunate Side Effects of Opiate Use

Medical research has made such progress, that there are practically no healthy people any more. – Aldous Huxley

Most opiate addicts don't take a long-term view of what they are doing to their bodies. Sadly, the effects can be far-reaching and sometimes unrecoverable. When using opiates is large amounts, there are few addicts who won't share stories of the unexpected physical and emotional changes that these drugs ushered into their lives. Opioid Induced Constipation is just one of these.

Opioid Induced Constipation (OIC) was introduced to the world in 2016 through a Super Bowl ad hawking a drug promising a "cure." It's been a fact of life for opiate addicts forever. In the aftermath of the ad, it was estimated that over 8 million people on prescription opiates are suffering from OIC, and these numbers are probably not taking into account the illicit users and heroin addicts. The bottom line, pun intended, is that if you are taking opiates on a regular basis, you are likely going to be severely constipated. I experienced this firsthand and had no idea that it was a "thing" until I got clean.

Another potential long-term effect of opiate use is a potential change in brain chemistry, which may or may not heal over time. This could have an effect on a person's pain tolerance, mood, libido, and cognitive functioning. As a recovering addict myself, I can say that I am much better off today than I was when I was using and I have witnessed many people recover completely who could scarcely string a sentence together when they first detoxed. Things do get better, but you have to put down the drugs for this to happen.

Other potential side effects of long-term use should you decide not to stop include:

- Reduced fertility

- Immune system depletion

- Irregular menses (women)

- Testosterone depletion (men)

- Intestinal damage

- Liver damage

Pain Pills and Painkiller Addiction

The priority of any addict is to anesthetize the pain of living to ease the passage of day with some purchased relief. — Russell Brand

Painkiller addiction and addiction to prescription medication gets a lot of headlines from the Hollywood crowd. No doubt it cuts across all boundaries. Whether you are a superstar, Fortune 500 executive, suburban housewife or teenager - this one tackles you and torments both physically and emotionally, whether in the spotlight or behind closed doors, and will take everything in the end. Sadly, Federal statistics show upwards of 2 million people in the grip of opiate addiction. Every 19 minutes, someone dies from a prescription painkiller overdose. In fact, the number of painkiller overdose deaths now exceeds the number of deaths from heroin and cocaine combined. Once thought, and even advertised, as having a "minimal risk of addiction" we now know better.

"It turns out that the doctors didn't know what they were talking about," said Barbara Howard, whose daughter Leslie, a home-care nurse, died of an overdose in 2009 in this small Appalachian town devastated by the epidemic. She had developed a habit after knee surgery. She left behind a 9-year-old son. "Leslie trusted the doctors. We thought the doctors knew what was best. But they didn't. We — and lots of the other victims — had no warning."

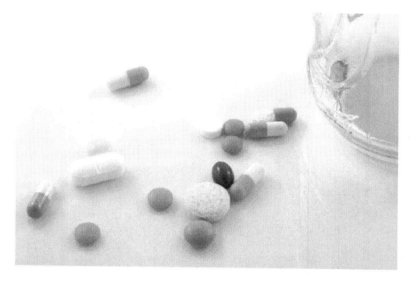

Retail prescriptions for opiate painkillers have tripled in the past 20 years, indicating that the rising sales and addictions were spurned by the massive effort to shape medical opinion and practice.   Drug manufacturers and some pain specialists bankrolled studies that helped create a body of scientific "evidence" appeasing the long-standing worries about opiates and pushed to expand their use for patients with chronic pain, including those with bad backs, arthritis, and sore knees. These studies reported minimal risk of addiction and were accepted by the nation's medical journals and even the FDA.   Medical boards relaxed rules for prescribing opiates and old fears of addiction and dependence were dismissed.

As it turns out, many of these studies were funded by Purdue Pharma, the maker of OxyContin, or other such drug manufacturers.   Also, many of the doctors whose conclusions were used had financial relationships with Purdue and other drug makers. Add to this the fact that, once thoroughly examined by the FDA, many of the claims and conclusions in the studies were not really supported by the data themselves. In fact, according to SAMSHA's 2012 National Survey on Drug Use and Health, some 6.8 million Americans abuse prescriptions pills.

Surprised? I hope not. Why throw you all of these drug policy facts and figures? Good question. I think it's important to know how we got here and to understand that, just because it's written in a medical journal or a physician said it, it's not necessarily true. History shows that these substances are highly addictive and prone to abuse. This isn't about placing blame or vengeance either because that would be counter-productive. An addict's first inclination is to look for something "official" that tells them it's ok to continue to do what they want to do. What I'm telling you here is - don't believe it. Painkillers are highly addictive in any way, shape or form - regardless of the official sway of opinion at any given moment in time.

Vicodin Addiction

Why do I act like I'm all high and mighty when inside I'm dying. I've finally realized that I need help. -Eminem

Find yourself addicted to Vicodin? You are not alone. In fact, you can join the ranks of such celebrities as Eminem, Jamie Lee Curtis, Brett Favre, Walter Payton, Matthew Perry, Nicole Richie and yours truly - though my level of celebrity status is debatable. I don't know about you, but something about inserting my name into this list gives me comfort. It drives home the fact that this really can happen to anyone, that recovery is possible, and that I can hold my head up and look people in the eye again someday.

Vicodin is a highly addictive drug, and Americans love it. The U.S., with just 5% of the world's population, now accounts for 99% of hydrocodone (Vicodin) consumption. Vicodin was classified as a Schedule III controlled substance when I (and those listed above) were consuming copious amounts of it, meaning that it has the potential for abuse and may lead to significant dependence. However, as of August 2014, the drug has been re-classified to a Schedule II, meaning that it now has tighter restrictions.

Vicodin is a combination of hydrocodone (the opiate) and acetaminophen (like Tylenol), for the relief of moderate to severe pain. Vicodin may contain 5 milligrams of hydrocodone and 325 milligrams of acetaminophen or as much as 10 milligrams of hydrocodone and 660 milligrams of acetaminophen. While hydrocodone is the addictive component of this pill, acetaminophen has resulted in serious liver damage at high dosages. Taking 2 grams of acetaminophen is considered a high dosage, so a person abusing Vicodin by taking a larger dosage than recommended is not only risking addiction to the opiate hydrocodone but also liver failure from the acetaminophen.

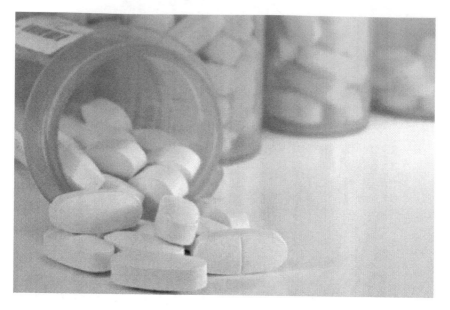

Vicodin will get you hooked, plain and simple. Its use changes the function of a critical area of your brain known as the mesolimbic dopamine system, frequently called the reward pathway. This reward pathway can be thought of as your "happy place." This area is responsible for feelings of euphoria but also for everyday feelings of pleasure and well-being. When a drug changes this pathway so much, it ceases to function properly on its own, and the user needs the drug simply to feel "normal."

It is possible to take Vicodin according to a prescription, i.e., - as medically necessary, and become physically dependent on it but not addicted to it. There is a difference. If you are increasing your dose on your own, i.e., - taking more than prescribed, crushing pills to chew or snort, or injecting the drug, you have crossed into addiction territory. Some Vicodin addiction symptoms include:

- Appearing drowsy or "nodding out."

- An obsession with procuring and consuming Vicodin

- An inability to focus on a given task

- Extreme anxiety and paranoia

- Severe mood swings

- Nausea and vomiting

Above all else, the obsession with getting more of the drug becomes first and foremost in the Vicodin addicts life. This was certainly the case for me as I turned to every means I could come up with, all fraudulent and most illegal, to procure more and more of the drug. I doctor shopped, I lied, I manipulated, and I committed prescription fraud over and over again. Actions that would normally horrify us in a right state of mind become commonplace and justified as a means to "survive." It took many years and a lot of consequences for me to throw in the towel and ask for help. Was this something that I could have done sooner? Sure - but I was in such a dark place that I really thought that my situation was "unique" and that there was no hope for me. I was wrong. There is a way out of Vicodin addiction, and I did not find it to be nearly as painful or tormenting as I had made my life up until that point. Active addiction is exhausting, and no one needs to live this way. If this is currently your life or that of a loved one, keep reading. There is a way out.

Oxycodone Addiction

*Selling my soul would be a lot easier if I could
just find it. — Nikki Sixx, The Heroin Diaries*

While under the pull of addiction, it's always nice to know that we're not alone. In fact, it gave me great solace to know that my demons were shared, not only by hundreds of thousands of others but by some rich and famous names as well. So, if OxyContin has you in its grip, perhaps it helps to know that it had also gotten its grimy claws into the likes of Rush Limbaugh, Heath Ledger, Courtney Love, Cindy Hensley-McCain, Winona Ryder, and Steven Tyler. These actors, rock stars, and almost-first lady were taken down just as ruthlessly as most addicts and suffered dire consequences as a result of their addictions. Courtney Love lost custody of her child, Winona racked up a slew of legal consequences all in the public eye, and Heath Ledger paid the ultimate sacrifice with his life.

The active ingredient in OxyContin is Oxycodone. Oxycodone is an opiate derived from morphine and is legally prescribed for pain relief. The prescription drug OxyContin is a Schedule II narcotic analgesic and is highly addictive. OxyContin was introduced in 1996 and has escalated in abuse ever since. Street terms for OxyContin are: OC, OX, Oxy, Oxycotton, Hillbilly heroin, and kicker. OxyContin, the most popular and well-known formulation of Oxycodone, is manufactured by Purdue Pharma. Purdue's formulation was a time-release pill and it was designed to last longer than other drugs but also to prevent abuse. How wrong they were as it turned to be very easy to get around this mechanism to experience the drug's full effects immediately, which are said to be similar to using heroin.

We use prescription opiates at alarming levels. According to an article published by the Pain Physician Journal in 2007, Americans use 80 percent of the world's supply of opioids and 84% of its oxycodone. "Sales of painkillers reached about $8.5 billion last year, compared with $4.4 billion in 2001, according to the consulting firm IMS Health," reported in a recent New York Times article. OxyContin was, and continues to be, a godsend for people in severe debilitating pain such as those with bone or neurological degeneration, or those suffering from end-stage cancer or similar illnesses. The drug provides pain relief to some who have suffered for a very long time. For others, it is the mere tip of the iceberg to a very dark and lonely place.

The physical and emotional signs and symptoms of using both OxyContin and heroin are very similar. While OxyContin is prescribed to treat pain, it does so by affecting the chemical pathway in the brain known as the dopamine pathway. Dopamine is the natural chemical in the brain that prepares us to experience good things like pleasure and a sense of well-being. Oxycodone floods those pathways with dopamine, and the user can experience feelings of euphoria and extreme happiness. However, as the body adjusts its internal chemistry over time, higher doses must be taken to feel the same result and then to even feel "normal."

Many people start off taking OxyContin legitimately for pain. There is a fine line between becoming physically dependent upon a drug and becoming addicted to it. However, consider this: if you are deciding when and how much of the drug to take and are taking it for the effect rather than for the pain relief, you have likely crossed that line. Abusers of OxyContin often exhibit such signs and symptoms as drowsiness, lightheadedness, itching, nausea, constipation, low blood pressure, respiratory suppression, headache, dry mouth, constricted pupils and sweating. Here are some other indications of OxyContin addiction:

- Chew OxyContin to prevent controlled release

- Crush OxyContin into a powder and either inject or snort OxyContin

- Take OxyContin in higher doses than prescribed

- Take OxyContin more frequently than prescribed

- Continued OxyContin abuse despite negative consequences

- Craving OxyContin and using it compulsively

- Seeking OxyContin to quickly affect the "reward center" of their brains

Overdose and even death can occur from OxyContin abuse due to respiratory suppression, particularly when it is combined with another drug that suppresses respiration, such as another opiate, benzos or alcohol.

One story of Oxy addiction illustrates this skyrocketing trend all too well. Mary, who is 16, is a voracious reader and a talented musician in her high school orchestra. She also admits to being a "garbage head," meaning that she will ingest anything she thinks will give her a high. Last December, she was taken to the hospital for an overdose of hallucinogenic mushrooms, alcohol, and ketamine, a chemical cousin of angel dust that doctors sometimes use to anesthetize patients and that, more commonly, veterinarians use to sedate large animals. Lately, she has been playing with one of the strongest opiates and potentially addictive painkillers ever created, OxyContin. She downs a few with a single shot of vodka and calls the combination "the sorority girl's diet cocktail," because it simultaneously allows for a stronger kick of inebriation and far fewer calories than mere alcohol alone. So where does this physically robust teenager obtain her pills? Weeks earlier, she had a tonsillectomy, a minor though uncomfortable procedure by any standards. The surgeon wrote a prescription for 80 tablets. Mary spent the next week in a narcotized and medically sanctioned bliss until her mother confiscated the last 20 tablets.

OxyContin addiction is very powerful, and those affected by it can attest to the fact that an addict will generally stop at nothing to get a hold of their next dose of drugs. Whether they need to steal it, buy from dealers, doctor-shop, or commit prescription fraud, the prescription drug addict finds themselves doing things that they never dreamed they would do in order to satisfy their cravings and prevent withdrawal symptoms from setting in. OxyContin is not, in fact, abused in quite the numbers that it was in the past. This is because, in 2010, the FDA required Purdue Pharma to reformulate the drug to make it harder to abuse. The newer version is designed so that it cannot be crushed or dissolved as was once the case. It can, however, still be abused by simply consuming greater quantities of it at once. As such, many OxyContin addicts have moved on to other opiates, including heroin.

Regardless, if you continue to use OxyContin or any other opiate and can't stop, there is a way out. Withdrawal and detox are part of the solution but detox from opiates is rarely life threatening, and you face bigger problems if you continue to do what you're doing. Recovery from prescription drug addiction is not only possible, it is within reach, and it is achieved all the time. All you need is a beginning and some good support to get started.

Percocet Addiction

Pain could be killed. Sadness could not, but the drugs did shut its mouth for a time. — Colson Whitehead

Percocet is a trade name for a prescription pain medication that combines oxycodone and acetaminophen. Oxycodone is an opiate analgesic, a narcotic derived from the same source as morphine and heroin. Percocet is generally prescribed for pain that is moderate to severe, short-term in nature and not typically used for chronic pain. The drug is produced in a variety of strengths, but most forms of Percocet contain between 2.5 and 10mg of oxycodone and 325 to 650 mg of acetaminophen, and both active ingredients reduce pain.

A popular drug that has seen a resurgence in the past few years is referred to on the streets as "Perc 30s." These are, in fact, not Percocet because they don't contain acetaminophen and Percocet doesn't come in 30mg tablets. They are straight Oxycodone tablets, aka roxicodone. These are also sometimes referred to as "roxys" or "blueberries" because of their color. Perc 30's skyrocketed in popularity soon after Perdue Pharma put out their tamper resistant formulation of OxyContin. Percocet and oxycodone are regulated as Schedule II narcotics under the Controlled Substances Act because it has a high potential for abuse. A Schedule II classification is the highest level of control for an FDA approved drug. In fact, physical addiction to Percocet can develop in as little as a week of continued use.

There are no direct statistics on Percocet abuse alone. However, according to the 2008 NSDUH, treatment admissions for abuse of prescription drugs increased fourfold in just ten years. The 2011 Monitoring the Future study conducted by the University of Michigan, documents the alarming increase in pain medication abuse in teens. Over 70 percent of seniors in high school who report using pain medication to get high obtained the pills for free from family and friends. Over 20 percent took the medication from their home medicine cabinets. Teens are abusing Percocet and other pain pills at pharm parties, where kids gain access to a variety of prescription pills in alarming combinations they call "trail mix."

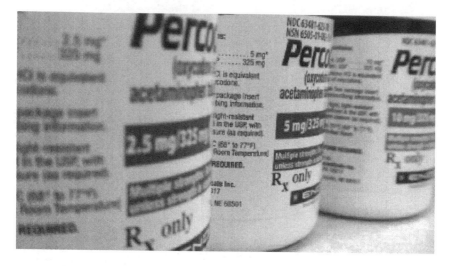

Prescription opioids such as Percocet are also widely over-prescribed, a driving factor for the abuse of the drug. The active opioid in the drug, oxycodone is produced en mass, and the International Narcotics Control Board estimates that 11.5 tons of oxycodone was manufactured worldwide in 1998, and by 2007, this figure had grown to 75.2 tons. The United States uses the most oxycodone worldwide, and in 2007 consumed an estimated 51.6 tons of the drug or 84% of the world total. This means that Americans consume over half a billion 80 mg tablets per year. So it isn't just a problem of illicit abuse, even the legitimate sale of Percocet is big business for drug companies, doctors, and pharmacies.

Percocet has a strong effect on the central nervous system (CNS), which is why it is so frequently abused. In high doses, the oxycodone produces a euphoric effect similar to a heroin high. In fact, drugs like Percocet have been referred to as the "White Collar heroin" because their use is less stigmatized than those of street drugs. The oxycodone in the drug is designed to be "time-released" but addicts looking for a more immediate high may bypass this function by chewing the pills before swallowing them, crushing them and putting them in a liquid and even diluting it to inject it directly into their bloodstream. Any and all of these methods are extremely dangerous and puts the individual at risk of overdose and even death.

Effects and side effects of Percocet abuse include constipation, memory loss, fatigue, dizziness, nausea, anxiety, headache, loss of appetite, dry mouth, abdominal pain, and diarrhea. Percocet has also been shown to cause lowered testosterone secretion, enlarged prostate, and impotence. In very high doses or when an overdose occurs, the user may suffer from clammy skin, hypotensia, respiratory arrest, circulatory collapse, low respiratory rates and even death. Oxycodone and taking dangerously high levels of acetaminophen can result in damage to kidneys and the liver.

While it is possible to become physically dependent on Percocet while taking it as prescribed, there is a fine line between this and crossing over into Percocet addiction. However, if you are taking larger doses than prescribed or are trying to achieve euphoric effects from the drug, you are misusing it, and addiction is a very real possibility. Some of the signs of Percocet addiction are:

- You need Percocet to deal with the normal stresses of everyday life

- Continued Percocet abuse despite negative consequences

- Craving Percocet and using it compulsively

- Seeking Percocet to stimulate the "reward center" of the brain

Overdose and death are very real concerns with Percocet addiction. Not only are you at risk from high doses of oxycodone, but overdose from acetaminophen has become more and more common. The acetaminophen found in many of these prescription painkillers is processed exclusively by the liver and can result in hepatotoxicity in very high doses, leading to death. This is particularly true when these drugs are taken in conjunction with alcohol, which is fairly commonplace. The combination can cause serious damage, oftentimes permanent, to the liver, kidneys and wall of the stomach. So much so that in 2009, the FDA recommended that Percocet, Vicodin and other narcotics containing acetaminophen be limited in sales due to the nearly 400 acetaminophen related deaths in the U.S. each year. I can personally attest to this as I have lasting stomach damage from my addiction that requires daily medication, despite being away from these drugs for a dozen years.

A woman named Bethany said she turned her life around after beating an addiction to prescription Percocet. She later turned to scoring it off the streets, which is why she went to jail twice. "I'm not so far away from it that I'm removed from it," Bethany said. "It's an everyday struggle and battle that I have to deal with."

Percocet's popularity has surged in 2016, and this potent drug has gotten plenty of press as the deadly drug of choice of Prince. Prince died of a prescription drug overdose on April 21, 2016, just hours before he was scheduled to begin treatment for opiate addiction. His death came on the heels of an overdose incident, and it's reported that he had been battling opiate addiction for many years. Again, this disease does not discriminate.

Percocet addiction is powerful, and it can be difficult if next to impossible, to quit on one's own once stuck in this endless cycle. There are withdrawal symptoms to contend with and intense craving for the drug. Once free of the drug, it can be difficult to remain clean without help and support. There is a way out, however, and it is immensely easier than the endless cycle of drug seeking and negative consequences. A life free from addiction to Percocet is absolutely possible.

Taite Adams

Morphine Addiction

End-stage addiction is mostly about waiting for the police, or someone, to come and bury you in your shame. — David Carr

Morphine is a naturally occurring opiate analgesic. It was first isolated in 1804 by Friedrich Serturner and then distributed in 1817. Widespread usage of morphine spread after the 1853 invention of the hypodermic needle. Morphine is the most abundant alkaloid found in the natural opium plant and is prescribed for relief of severe pain and suffering. Morphine is found on the street by the names of morf, M, sister morphine, Vitamin M, morpho, Miss Emma and dreamer, amongst others. With a prescription, morphine costs around $25 per injection of 4cc in the hospital. On the street morphine prices vary but tend to cost $35-$40 per 100mg pill. Morphine is classed a Schedule II drug in the United States, meaning it has medical use but is illegal for recreational use and is highly susceptible to abuse. Morphine comes in the form of either capsules, tablets, or taken via intravenous injection.

Morphine was first used medicinally as a painkiller and, erroneously, as a cure for opium addiction. Morphine quickly replaced opium as a cure-all recommended by doctors and as a recreational drug and was readily available from drugstores or through the mail. Substitution of Morphine addiction for alcohol addiction was at one time considered beneficial by some physicians because alcohol was seen as more destructive to the body and more likely to trigger antisocial behavior. Morphine was used during the American Civil War as a surgical anesthetic and was sent home with many wounded soldiers for the relief of pain. At the end of the war, over 400,000 people had the "army disease", i.e., - Morphine addiction. The Franco-Prussian War in Europe had a similar effect.

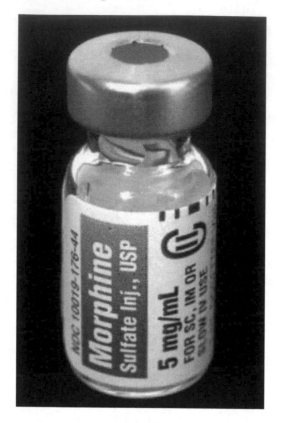

Morphine is the classic opiate painkiller, the standard by which other opiates are measured. Morphine, a narcotic, directly affects the central nervous system. Besides relieving pain, Morphine's effects impair mental and physical performance, relieve fear and anxiety, and produce euphoria. Morphine's effects also decrease hunger, inhibit the cough reflex, produce constipation, and usually reduce the sex drive; in women, it may interfere with the menstrual cycle. Morphine's euphoric effects can be highly addictive. Tolerance (the need for higher and higher doses to maintain the same effect) and physical and psychological dependence develop quickly.

Morphine is generally used to treat both acute and chronic severe pain. Morphine itself appears to mimic endorphins, which are responsible for reducing pain, causing sleepiness and feelings of pleasure. It interacts predominantly with the μ- opioid receptor in the central nervous system. Morphine, a rapid-acting narcotic, often has a higher incidence of euphoria, respiratory depression, sedation, tolerance, and physical and psychological dependence when compared with other opioids of equal doses.

Some additional side effects of taking morphine include dizziness, diarrhea, irritability, difficulty sleeping, shaking and difficulty urinating. Some of the more serious side effects of taking morphine, which also tend to indicate possible morphine abuse include shallow or irregular breathing, fast or slow heartbeat, seizures, hallucinations, fainting, hives/rash, difficulty swallowing and swelling of extremities.

In addition to the physical symptoms of abuse, there are behaviors and physical evidence that are generally believed to indicate morphine addiction. Pill bottles or syringes may be left lying around or haphazardly hidden. Morphine also comes in a liquid form so you may find small bottles of morphine sulfate liquid. There are dozens of different pills and capsules that contain morphine. By brand name, Avinza® capsules are half white, and the other half may be blue, dark green, light blue, yellow or red. Kadian® capsules are all one color and may be light blue, turquoise, purple, brown or pink, depending on the dosage. MS Contin® are small round pills in gray, light blue, purple, or orange. Oramorph® SR (sustained release) are round white pills but may also be supplied in a patch. Generic morphine comes in a variety of colors and shapes.

Morphine addiction is difficult to overcome as morphine creates thousands of nerve receptors in the brain which cause serious cravings 24/7 when not given more of the drug. Opiate addiction is a cruel master as the drugs cause strong cravings, strong enough to drive a person to commit acts he (or she) would never otherwise commit. A family may be torn apart as a person's true personality becomes hidden by the compulsions and manipulations required to continue the addiction. Recovery from morphine addiction is possible, however. The road to recovery starts with some form of opiate detox (read section on this) and then learning how to live life without the use of drugs. This is not only possible, but it's also infinitely easier than that of the day to day life a morphine addict.

Opiate Addiction

Hydromorphone Addiction

Addicts know no shame. You disgrace yourself
so many times you become immune to it.
— John Grisham, The Testament

Hydromorphone is a derivative of the morphine family and is most commonly known by its most popular brand name: Dilaudid. A very potent centrally acting analgesic of the opioid class, hydromorphone is commonly used (and abused) in a hospital setting as it is often administered intravenously (IV). Dilaudid is a Schedule II opioid that can be taken as an injection, tablet or suppository.

While derived from morphine, it would be a mistake to compare this drug to even this very powerful opiate, as hydromorphone is thought to be 6-9 times stronger than morphine and 3-5 times stronger than heroin. Hydromorphone is not a new drug by any means. First synthesized and researched in Germany in 1924, it was released to the mass market in 1926 under the name Dilaudid. However, its use and abuse have been growing exponentially in recent years. According to the DEA, 766 kilograms (1,688 pounds) of medically produced hydromorphone were manufactured in 1998. By 2006, this number had surged to 3,300 kilograms (7,275 pounds), an increase of over 330%.

In general, the effects and half-life of Dilaudid is very short. Due to its chemical structure, the drug has a higher lipid solubility and is able to cross the blood-brain barrier much more efficiently, creating a more drastic effect on the central nervous system. This means that the drug is faster-acting than many other opiates, is much more potent, and will wear off much more quickly. However, those who use the drug that also have underlying kidney problems are throwing extra caution to the wind as the half-life can build up, potentially resulting in death with continued use.

Because it's an opiate, the effects of Dilaudid are similar to many of those we've already covered, except oftentimes more intense due to the chemical makeup and metabolism of the drug. Dilaudid can produce feelings of euphoria, relaxation, pain relief and sedation. The user may feel a reduction in anxiety, have suppressed respiration and cough suppression. These are all short-term effects. Long-term use effects include rashes, urinary tract problems, anxiety, difficulty breathing, and fainting.

Because of its potency, Dilaudid is ripe for abuse. In fact, in the 1970's and 80's, the DEA listed Hydromorphone as a "leading opioid product for abuse and diversion." Between 1998 and 2006, hydromorphone prescriptions increased over 280%. Whether taking these drugs legally or not, people simply don't understand their potency. In 2006 alone, hydromorphone products sent over 6,700 people to the ER.

Because of its short half-life, withdrawal symptoms can begin in as little to 9 hours after the last dose. While detox may not last as long as with other opiates, it is quite intense, and the psychological cravings are nothing to shake a stick at. Formidable but not impossible, recovery from Dilaudid addiction is absolutely within reach for anyone who really wants it and is ready. Please read the chapters on Opiate Detox if this is your reality. There is hope.

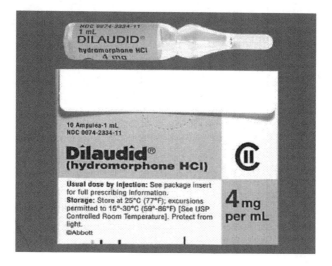

Fentanyl Addiction

*Imagine trying to live without air. Now imagine
something worse. — Amy Reed, Clean*

Fentanyl is similar to Hydromorphone (discussed in the last chapter) in that it is a very strong opiate and it is fast-acting. Actually, that's mostly where the similarities end. Fentanyl is incredibly potent, approximately 80-100 times stronger than morphine and much more than heroin. Also known by the brand names Sublimaze, Duragesic, Actiq and others, fentanyl is commonly used to treat breakthrough pain in conjunction with surgical procedures.

First synthesized by Paul Janssen in 1960, fentanyl first came under medical use with the trade name Sublimaze. In the mid-1990's, fentanyl saw a surge in widespread use with the development of the Duragesic patch and later the Actiq lollipop. As a Schedule II prescription drug, fentanyl has many important medical uses, such as for anesthesia and pain relief. Often used for the management of chronic pain, including cancer pain, fentanyl transdermal patches work by releasing the drug into the bloodstream over 48 to 72 hours. Dosage and rate of absorption vary depending upon a number of factors.

Because one of these fentanyl patches essentially carries enough narcotics for up to 3 days, they are ripe for abuse, particularly from those who have figured out how to extract those multiple days worth of the drug into a single dose. Those who abuse fentanyl patches usually employ one of the following to rapidly ingest high amounts of the drug:

- Applying multiple patches to the body at one time

- Eating or sucking on a patch

- Smoking the gel from a patch

- Extracting the drug from a patch and injecting with a hypodermic needle

As with most other opiates, the main effects of fentanyl use are euphoria, drowsiness, and lethargy. Abused and taken in high doses, you can expect to experience: dry mouth, urine retention, breathing suppression, severe constipation, itching, nausea and vomiting, loss of appetite, depression, sleep disturbances, sweating, and hallucinations. Because fentanyl is so powerful, and this isn't understood by many who try it, unconsciousness, coma, and death also occur.

Make no mistake; this is a deadly opiate. In July 2005, the U.S. Food and Drug Administration responded to reports of hundreds of fentanyl-related deaths by issuing a public health advisory regarding the use of fentanyl skin patches. Noting that it continued to receive reports of fatal and near-fatal responses to improper use of the patches, the FDA released a December 2007 update that stressed the severity of complications associated with fentanyl abuse:

The fentanyl patch contains ... a very potent narcotic pain medicine. It is only intended for treating persistent, moderate to severe pain in patients who are opioid-tolerant, meaning those patients who take a regular, daily, around-the-clock narcotic pain medicine. ... For patients who are not opioid-tolerant, the amount of fentanyl in one fentanyl patch of the lowest strength is large enough to cause dangerous side effects, such as respiratory depression (severe trouble breathing or very slow or shallow breathing) and death.

Fentanyl patches, even when used and discarded, are still potent and extremely dangerous. Addicts seek them out, and they have been the source of injury, and even death, in children. In July 2014, the Medicines and Healthcare Products Regulatory Agency (MHRA) issued a warning about the potential harm, particularly to children, from exposure to fentanyl patches. Detailed "Instructions for Use", including information on disposal, is available on the FDA website.

Both fentanyl and a new opioid analgesic called Acetyl fentanyl are now being mixed with heroin and users are, either knowingly or not, being exposed to these very powerful opiates that their bodies and brains may not be able to handle. In 2006, non-pharmaceutical fentanyl mixed with heroin caused an outbreak of overdose deaths in the United States, mainly concentrated in the cities of Chicago, Detroit, Philadelphia, Baltimore, Pittsburgh, and St. Louis. This mixture is known as "magic" or "the bomb" on the street.

Historically, Fentanyl came in patches which were easily defeated. While there are mechanisms in place to make patches more difficult to abuse, they aren't foolproof. Yet, the fentanyl of today is often found in pill form as well, and many addicts aren't even aware that they're receiving this deadly opiate. In Sacramento, it's been reported that fentanyl has been pressed into pill form and sold as Norco, a much less potent painkiller. In just one month's time in 2016, there were 48 overdoses and 12 deaths in Northern California attributed to fentanyl. Deaths and overdoses are piling up and, because the users oftentimes have no idea what they've taken, treatment becomes difficult. It turns out that a standard dose of Naloxone will not be effective for someone that has overdosed on this powerful drug.

In June 2013, The U.S. Centers for Disease Control and Prevention (CDC) issued a health advisory to emergency departments with regards to 14 overdose deaths among IV drug users in Rhode Island associated with Acetyl fentanyl. This is a non-classified synthetic opioid analog of fentanyl, and what would be considered by most a "research chemical." There are other fentanyl analogs, such as a-methylfentanyl (AMF), also referred to as "China White", that are now classed as Schedule I drugs. News stories about fentanyl have spiked once again 2016 as the death toll from this drug alone has gone through the roof. In 2015 alone, fentanyl killed 158 people in the state of New Hampshire and over 300 people in neighboring Massachusetts.

Addiction to fentanyl can happen quick and is brutal. The addict's life quickly deteriorates around them, as friends and family get fed up and disappear. Unethical and even criminal acts become commonplace in an effort to feed a never-ending hunger for more. Every aspect of life becomes secretive and, eventually, hopeless.

If you or a loved one is addicted to fentanyl, there is hope. Many have recovered and will be there to share their stories with you. While detox from fentanyl can be severe, it is generally not dangerous. Be sure to read about The Disease Concept and A Way Out for the Opiate Addict as you move forward.

Tramadol Addiction

There is nothing more deceptive than an obvious fact. — *Arthur Conan Doyle*

Tramadol, also known by its brand name Ultram, is an opioid pain medication that has become widely dispensed over recent years to treat moderate pain for a variety of issues. Available as an immediate release tablet (50 mg) or as an extended release tablet (100, 200, or 300 mg), Tramadol has often been mistaken for an NSAID in the past, but it definitely is not. I have called this drug a "sleeping giant" for many years because it almost took me back out after having been clean and sober for over five years.

I suffered a minor, yet painful, injury to my shoulder and went to a family physician to have it looked at. He prescribed some exercises, ice and handed me a prescription for Ultram. I had made my history with opiates crystal clear and asked him if this was a "controlled substance." He, rightly, told me that it was not so I got it filled and began taking it. What I found, even when taking the medication as prescribed, was that I liked the feeling that it gave me and I wanted more. This frightened me enough to stop taking it, and I didn't understand the insidiousness of this drug until I researched it many years later.

It turns out that, back in 2005 when this occurred, Tramadol was not listed under the Controlled Substance Act, so anyone with a prescription pad could (and did) prescribe it. In fact, more than 26 million prescriptions were dispensed in 2008 alone, many from nurse practitioners, physician's assistants, family practice physicians, and osteopaths. That number had risen to 40 million in 2012, according to data from IMS Health, a market research firm.

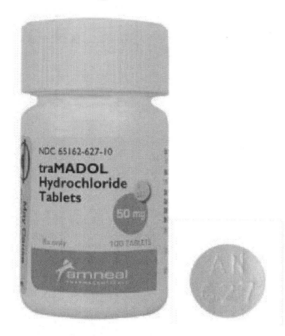

Tramadol was first introduced in Germany in 1977. It took another 20 years before it was launched in the United States and the UK. The FDA approved Tramadol in the U.S. for the drug company Janssen Pharmaceuticals under the brand name Ultram. As of 2002, there is also a generic on the market. When first introduced in the U.S., apparently too much of the German data was used as a means for classification. Data from German studies showed that Tramadol was only about one-tenth as potent as morphine and that it had very little potential for abuse. Wrong on both counts.

In the early 1990's, Johns Hopkins did a study on Tramadol in which high doses were given to opioid abusers. At these doses, the drug produced effects much like a high dose of oxycodone. While this study wasn't published, the findings were provided to the FDA, who still approved the drug as a non-controlled substance. The company that initially marketed Ultram, Ortho-McNeill, did so with the strategy that it be kept off the controlled substances list so that it wouldn't have to compete with other narcotic painkillers.

As early as 2006, there were arguments springing up that Tramadol should be made a controlled substance. Ortho-McNeill continued to fight these efforts, arguing that by making it a controlled substance, doctors would be less likely to prescribe it for chronic pain. They cited concerns about the stigma attached to opioids and called it "opiophobia." These comments were made in a document filed with the FDA in response to an inquiry by the World Health Organization over whether Tramadol should become a scheduled narcotic internationally.

If there is a question about whether or not a drug is ripe for abuse, simply take a look at the sheer number of those who are using it recreationally. Profound stuff, right? In 2011 alone, 2.6 million people ages 12 and older used Tramadol for nonmedical purposes, according to the DEA. Also per the DEA, this drug is most commonly abused by addicts, chronic pain patients, and health professionals.

Tramadol isn't just being abused by patients and health professionals, however. In fact, police across the country say teens can get Tramadol more easily than alcohol. While Tramadol has an extended released (ER) product, this doesn't matter as it isn't protected against abuse as some other drugs are. Crushing and injecting Tramadol, whether the extended release version or not, often produces the same instant euphoric effects as heroin, morphine, and oxycontin. With abuse comes overdose and, usually, reported deaths.

The Drug Abuse Warning Network (DAWN) is a federally operated, national surveillance system that monitors trends in drug-related emergency room visits. Over the period from 1995 to 2002, DAWN reported more than 12,000 cases of emergency room visits mentioning Tramadol. Tramadol case numbers increased significantly (165%) during this time. And people are dying from taking this drug. Deaths from Tramadol overdose have skyrocketed from just one in 1996 to 154 in 2011 alone. Between 2006 and 2011, more than 500 people died from Tramadol overdoses.

As the seriousness of the abuse potential for this drug became something that could no longer be ignored, the FDA finally took action two years ago (2014). Effective, August 18, 2014, Tramadol has been placed into Schedule IV of the federal Controlled Substances Act.

In addition to this (and much prior to), several states and the U.S. Military have already classified Tramadol as a schedule IV controlled substance under state law. These states are Arkansas, Georgia, Kentucky, Illinois, Mississippi, New York, North Dakota, Ohio, Oklahoma, Tennessee, West Virginia, and Wyoming. The drug is also now a Schedule 3 in the UK as of June 2014.

If you unwittingly, or even knowingly, have gotten yourself hooked on Tramadol, know that you are not alone. This is a drug that nearly pulled me in as well, and it wasn't a pleasant experience knowing that I had been taking these and falling under their spell. Detox and withdrawal from Tramadol can vary depending on how much and how long you used the drug for. More severe withdrawal symptoms are generally felt when discontinuing from a lengthy use at a high daily dose. It is also possible to use some form of tapering method before initiating detox. Tramadol withdrawal can last a bit longer than other opiates because there is an anti-depressant component to the drug that you are also withdrawing from. Regardless, withdrawal is generally not dangerous, and you can find more information about withdrawal, tapering and recovery options further on in the book.

Zohydro and Its Dangers

No matter how bad things are, you can always make things worse. - Randy Pausch

One of the reasons we are in our 4th edition of this book, aside from correcting a few typos, is to bring you some up to date information about Opiate Addiction and any new drugs on the market that may be of concern. This one is a whopper.

In October 2013, the FDA approved this new hydrocodone-based drug, which is slated to "treat chronic pain" and was released on the market in March 2014 before being promptly pulled back amid an outraged public. This was just one day after they made the front page of the New York Times for responsibly announcing that they were recommending moving drugs like Vicodin to Schedule II to make them harder to access. If this is done, patients can no longer receive automatic refills and physicians can no longer phone in prescriptions.

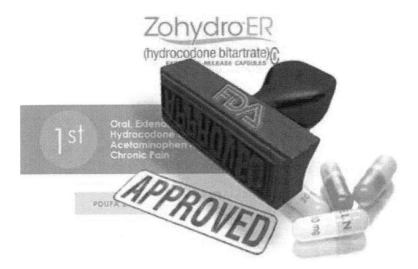

While Zohydro was briefly an "approved" Schedule II drug, don't think for one minute that it is safe. The medication is an extended-release painkiller that is pure hydrocodone (no aspirin or acetaminophen) and uses a higher dosage scale than the hydrocodone-combo drugs like Vicodin. Just one pill of Zohydro can pack the punch of 5 to 10 Vicodin. It's so strong, experts say, that someone new to opioids could die from just two pills. Just think of what one of these could do to a child. The maker of Zohydro has come under considerable fire because this drug has no mechanisms built-in that are abuse-deterrents. In fact, they come in capsules which are so prone to abuse it's laughable.

Why was this drug ever approved? No idea, really. Big pharma, again. Several groups of "experts" were successful in their appeal to the FDA to reconsider their approval, with letters, petitions, and legislation in some States. More than 40 experts wrote one letter to the FDA -- "In the midst of a severe drug addiction epidemic fueled by overprescribing of opioids, the very last thing the country needs is a new, dangerous, high-dose opioid," the experts wrote, addressing FDA Commissioner Margaret A. Hamburg, MD. One member of the letter-writing coalition, Andrew Kolodny, president of the advocacy group Physicians for Responsible Opioid Prescribing, was more blunt: "It's a whopping dose of hydrocodone packed in an easy-to-crush capsule. It will kill people as soon as it's released."

Zogenix, the makers of Zohyro, took so much slack for this particular drug that they bailed out of the game altogether. In 2015, the company sold the drug and all related R&D projects to New Jersey-based Permix Therapeutics for a healthy sum. At present, the new owners of the drug have to submit a tamper-resistant version to the FDA, something that should happen anytime. Meanwhile, Purdue Pharma's abuse-resistant Hysingla has been on the market for over a year. While these drugs are supposed to be resistant to abuse, they can be defeated. I'm not going to tell you how as that isn't the aim of this book.

Prescription Drug Abuse and Chronic Pain

It is during our darkest moments that we must focus to see the light. -Aristotle Onassis

While the U.S. may be a pioneer in wiping out chronic pain, it has created a monster with its byproduct of painkiller addiction. In fact, prescription drug overdoses are now killing upwards of 25,000 Americans per year, and the death toll continues to rise. This is triple the rate of just a decade ago, according to the CDC, which has now declared the problem to be an epidemic. In fact, the death toll exceeds that caused by heroin and cocaine combined, and in 17 States has become the Number 1 cause of injury deaths, surpassing even car crashes.

Going beyond the scale of the problem is the striking profile of many of the victims and where these drugs are originating. Advances in medicine over the years have left us to expect a great deal - a higher quality of life, cured diseases and freedom from pain. Thanks, in part, to erroneous advertising and questionable studies touting their safety, the level of prescription opiates being dolled out by physicians has soared, and with it the incidence of addiction.

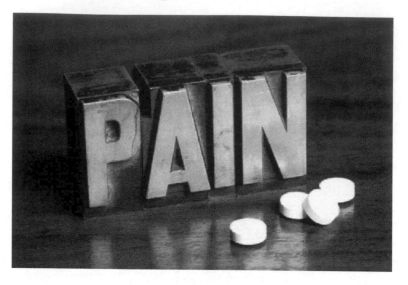

Modern views about the threat posed to patients by narcotics were shaped in the mid-1980's when pain treatment experts reported that cancer patients treated with such drugs did not exhibit the type of euphoria displayed by people who abused narcotics. That led some physicians to argue that strong, long-acting narcotics could also be used safely to treat patients with serious pain unrelated to cancer, like persistent back pain or nerve disorders.   Drug companies amplified these themes in materials sent to doctors and pharmacists. For example, Janssen Pharmaceutica, the producer of Duragesic, called the risk of addiction "relatively rare" in a package insert with the drug. Endo Pharmaceuticals termed the risk "very rare" in presentations to hospital pharmacists. Purdue Pharma, the manufacturer of the powerful narcotic OxyContin, distributed a brochure to chronic pain patients called "From One Pain Patient to Another," contending that it and similar drugs posed minimal risks.

Today, some narcotics manufacturers like Endo have changed or are changing the way they present abuse and addiction information. For example, Purdue Pharma, while maintaining the accuracy of its past position, now states in patient information that it does "not know how often patients with continuing (chronic) pain become addicted to narcotics but the risk has been reported to be small." Ligand Pharmaceuticals, which manufactures a time-released form of morphine under the brand name Avinza, makes a similar statement.

For its part, a spokeswoman for the federal Food and Drug Administration, Kathleen K. Quinn, said the agency believed that "the risk of addiction to chronic pain patients treated with narcotic analgesics has not been well studied and is not well characterized."

What is clear is this - there is, indeed, a very real risk of addiction with these drugs. Whether it be an iatrogenic addiction (accidental) or not as a result of taking prescription opiates at high doses, it doesn't really matter. Once addicted, it's all the same. In fact, the notion that patients (or users) began taking these pills for a legitimate pain issue doesn't often do them any favors. What it does do is give them a so-called rationale to keep using at whatever levels they feel necessary and, most of the time, leaves them with an untreated pain issue. Sounds maddening, doesn't it?

These prescription pain meds physically affect the body to the point that you are much worse off than when you started taking them. Here's what happens:

- The brain responds to the pain medicine by increasing the number of receptors for the drug, and the nerve cells in the brain stop functioning

- The body stops producing endorphins (the body's natural painkillers) because it is receiving opiates instead

- The degeneration of the nerve cells in the brain causes a physical dependency on an external supply of opiates and reducing or not taking the painkillers causes a painful series of physical changes, known as withdrawal.

- At this point, many people (an estimated 7% who are prescribed narcotic analgesics) continue taking the pain medication to avoid the withdrawal symptoms rather than to treat the original pain.

If that isn't bad enough, what most people don't realize (I didn't), is that taking prescription painkillers over a period of time can result in what's called hyperalgesia, where you become increasingly sensitive to pain. So, essentially your pain gets WORSE because you have taken these drugs to excess. This happens because long-term use of opiate painkillers causes a decrease in your ability to tolerate pain and an increased sensitivity to pain. When the pain increases, people are often led to believe they need to take higher doses of pain medication than they were on initially. Unfortunately, it just stops working, and there is never enough. That's why we hear of people taking absolutely obscene amounts of opiates that would generally kill a herd of rhinos. I was taking handfuls of painkillers at a time to manage what, in the beginning, was moderate neck pain and headaches. In fact, the pain had increased to a level, some of it psychosomatic, that I truly believed I was dying. Once away from the pills for a time, however, I was astounded to find that my pain had essentially disappeared.

So what's the solution for those with chronic pain? There are differing views on this. If you are already addicted to opiate painkillers, it will be a very tall order for you to be able to go back to taking any sort of opiate medication at manageable levels and likely a tolerance has developed that would make them quite ineffective. I am fifteen years away from opiates and still require a heavier dose of anesthetic or pain medications in the rare event that I must undergo an invasive procedure. This is because my brain chemistry has been altered to the point where I have a permanent tolerance for these drugs. Thankfully, for those with chronic pain issues, there are non-opiate pain management avenues that can be explored.

Patients with substance abuse issues can be treated for pain in a variety of ways that don't involve opioids, says Sean Mackey, MD, PhD, Chief of the Pain Management Division at Stanford University and Associate Professor of Anesthesia and Pain Management. "A multidisciplinary approach is needed to treat patients in pain who have substance abuse issues," he says. There are non-opioid drugs such as anti-epileptic drugs, antidepressants and anti-arrhythmic drugs, which can be effective in treating pain, Dr. Mackey says. Patients can also be treated with physical therapy, occupational therapy, combined with psychological therapies. If, however, an opioid treatment is still deemed necessary for someone with addiction issues, buprenorphine and methadone have been used in these instances, and both have strong analgesic (pain relieving) benefits. They also have addictive properties and downsides so be sure to do research on these and ask plenty of questions before you begin taking them.

What may have begun as an attempt to alleviate the pain from an accident, surgery or other condition has likely had unintended consequences and led to a prescription painkiller addiction. Regardless of how you got here, laying blame isn't going to get you very far. Once addicted to a substance, there is no turning back the clock to become "un-addicted" to it. Fortunately, this is a hole that, no matter how deep it may seem at the moment, you can crawl out of and begin to rebuild what these drugs have likely taken from you. If you do have legitimate pain issues that need to be managed, be sure to involve your trusted physicians in your decision to get clean and in deciding new avenues for treatment from this point forward. Nothing but complete honesty will work in this regard. This is the first step in recovery.

Numbing the pain for a while will make it worse when you finally feel it. — J.K. Rowling

Heroin Addiction Examined

Everything one does in life, even love, occurs in an express train racing toward death. To smoke opium is to get out of the train while it is still moving. It is to concern oneself with something other than life or death. -Jean Cocteau

Heroin (diacetylmorphine or morphine diacetate), also known asdiamorphine, is an opioid analgesic first synthesized by C.R. Alder Wright in 1874 by adding two acetyl groups to the molecule morphine, found in the opium poppy plant. It functions as a morphine pro-drug, meaning that it is metabolically converted to morphine inside the body in order for it to work. Street names for heroin include H, smack, horse, brown, black, tar, dope, brown sugar, muc, skag, among others.

Heroin is found in several forms but many times is a white to dark brown powder or tar-like substance. It can be used in a variety of ways as well depending on the users preference and the purity of the drug. It can be injected, smoked and snorted. A very short-acting opiate, effects appear soon after ingesting the drug and disappear in a few hours. Generally, there is a surge of euphoria with a warm flushing of the skin, dry mouth, and weighty extremities. Mental functioning will become clouded due to a depressed central nervous system, followed by drowsiness and possible nausea.

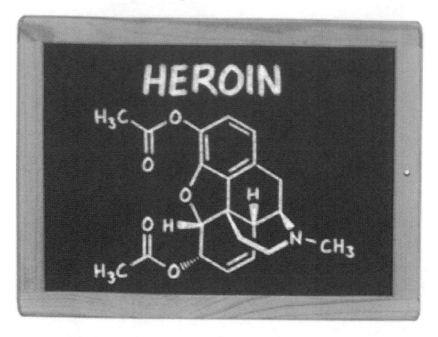

Heroin is an illegal substance, nearly everywhere, so its manufacture is not regulated by any governmental agency. Because of this, it is bought on the street, and the quality, purity and even appearance of the drug will vary. Many dealers will add other substances and even other drugs to heroin to dilute it, enhance it or change the product, all adding to the danger of overdose or poisoning deaths.

Long-term, heroin use can do a significant amount of damage to the user's body. For example, a study published in the journal Neuropsychopharmacology found that people who abuse heroin perform poorly on mental functioning tests. They have trouble recognizing patterns, dealing with spatial concepts and remembering details. These changes can also appear in brain scans, where the heroin addicts brain appears shrunken and inactive. People who inject heroin are subject to a wide variety of long-term health problems, including:

- Collapsed veins

- Abscesses

- Infections of the heart or lungs

- Blood-borne infections such as AIDS or hepatitis B and C

Heroin has gotten more air time than normal, and it gets a lot, due to the recent overdose death of actor Philip Seymour Hoffman from the drug. People seem to take more notice when a celebrity dies and are now shouting that "hey, this is a problem!". Well, yeah it is, but it's been a problem for some time now, and every death from heroin and opiates is an absolute tragedy.

Hardly anyone will disagree that heroin is a highly addictive opiate. What's alarming is its recent resurgence as a drug of choice in America in just the past several years. This is largely due to the mass numbers of prescription opiate addicts that are crossing over from pills to heroin. There is now little doubt that these painkillers are serving as a gateway to heroin addiction.

Why Most Opiate Addicts Turn to Heroin

Junk is the ideal product... the ultimate merchandise. No sales talk necessary. The client will crawl through a sewer and beg to buy. -William S. Burroughs

Ed's road to heroin abuse began with long drives across the Upper Midwest to find doctors and pharmacists he could scam for pain pills. He was first prescribed drugs like Tylenol 3 and Vicodin after a significant fall at a construction site in the early 1990s. Eventually, he started injecting crushed prescription opiates into his veins to get a stronger kick. "It got to the point where I was doing an incredible amount of those, and it was getting so cost prohibitive that I found it better to just turn around and sell the pills and buy heroin," he said. "Somewhere in the middle there, the line became blurred between pain relief and addiction."

A few years ago, Palm Beach County resident Karen Perry sent her son off to college, not knowing he'd gotten hooked first on oxycodone, and then something cheaper and stronger: heroin. "At some point, it became expensive to buy prescription pills, so he started buying heroin," she said, reflecting on her son's fatal overdose.

While just two stories, these are very indicative of a frightening new trend that is largely being fueled by a national crackdown on prescription painkillers. While many painkiller addicts think of heroin as a low-class drug that they would never touch, the reality is that they are already addicted to a form of it. Opiates act on the reward system of the brain and are highly addictive. When one is not available, generally, another will do to satisfy the cravings and keep withdrawal symptoms from setting in.

While access to prescription painkillers should absolutely be limited, as has been the case in recent years, it has had some unforeseen consequences in the explosion of heroin abuse. With new regulations and law enforcement making access to these drugs much more difficult, users are being driven to another opiate that happens to be cheaper, more powerful and infinitely more destructive. Always ready to oblige our hunger (basic economics), floods of cheap heroin continue to enter the country from Mexico and South America. Heroin use and abuse is now cropping up in cities, towns and upscale suburban communities that previously found its appearance rare. A SAMHSA study from August of 2012 found that people aged 12 to 49 who had abused prescription painkillers were 19 times more likely than those who hadn't to try heroin in the previous year. Last year, nearly 700,000 Americans took the drug, twice as many as a decade ago.

Heroin in Charlotte, NC has become so easy to get that dealers deliver to the suburbs and run specials to attract their young, professional, upper-income customers. These lawyers, nurses, cops and ministers are showing up in the detox ward at Carolinas Medical Center, desperate to kick an opiate addiction that often started with powerful prescription painkillers such as OxyContin and Vicodin. The center analyzed the patients' ZIP codes to find out where heroin had taken root, says Robert Martin, director of substance abuse services at the medical center. "Our heroin patients," he said, "come from the five best neighborhoods."

Heroin addiction is changing rapidly in this country, both geographically and demographically. When we think of painkiller addicts now, may times we think of housewife, professional, suburban teenager, and even the occasional retiree. Well take that mental picture and apply it to heroin addiction. More than two-thirds of heroin addicts have previously abused prescription painkillers. The pills have become expensive, and often hard to obtain. Prescription opiates now sell for anywhere from $30 to $80 a pill. A $10 bag of heroin offers a similar or better high. Unable to find pills, or afford them, addicts go looking for something else to feed the craving. Heroin is cheap, plentiful and potent.

"If you were to tell me that I was going to use heroin ... the same week in which I used it, I probably would have laughed in your face," said Tej Yaich, a 20-year-old from Pickerington, Ohio. "That's something that I would never have done." Tej, who has now been sober for more than a year, started his addiction at home. His parents had prescriptions sitting unused in the medicine cabinet. Yaich said he was 15 when he first tried them. The experiment became a habit. Then the supply started to dry up. One day I went to call my guy that was selling to me and he said he didn't have pills at that time, but he had something equally as good," said Yaich. "He said, 'You'll like it.'" What the dealer had was heroin, and he was right. Yaich started by snorting it, then quickly moved on to shooting up. From one bag, he worked himself up to two, then five. At the height of his addiction, he said, he injected up to 25 bags a day.

Economics have been mentioned several times in this book, and this always plays a part when it comes to the drug trade, and especially so with heroin. In recent years, the supply of heroin has gone up dramatically in response to market demand. Between 2000 and 2009, the amount of land in Mexico being used to grow opium poppies increased tenfold. As Americans are consuming less cocaine than in the past and nearly half of the states have legalized medical marijuana, drug exporters and domestic dealers have switched their allegiance to heroin. There is a very hungry market out there for the drug as the supply of prescription opioids continues to shift.

This cross-over happens very quickly and insidiously. Addictions take us to places that we thought we'd never go and lead us to do things we couldn't imagine doing in a right frame of mind. Heroin use is rife with danger and will always result in the piling up of negative consequences. Awareness of heroin's dangers is key if you are thinking of trying this or if you are living this now and want to find a way out.

Dangers and Consequences of Heroin Use

I've never had a problem with drugs. I've had problems with the police. -Keith Richards

Made from morphine, a substance found in the opium poppy plant, heroin is one of the most addictive drugs in circulation. A powerful narcotic, its potential for abuse is very high, and users can form both physical and psychological dependence on it. Heroin has gone in and out of style over the years, but its resurgence in popularity makes awareness of this drug, its effects and its dangers a must.

Under the Controlled Substances Act, heroin is classified as a Schedule I drug, meaning that it is highly addictive and not safe to use in a medical setting. This also means that it is manufactured on "the street" and often mixed with adulterants that can be almost as harmful as the heroin itself. Some of these additives may not readily dissolve and could result in clogged blood vessels that lead to the lungs, liver, kidneys or brain. This can cause infection, organ damage or even death. Most IV heroin users don't know exactly what they're shooting into their veins. According to the Metropolitan Police Department of Washington, D.C., some of the diluents that are added to street heroin include:

- Sugar or sugar substitutes

- Cornstarch or other starches

- Strychnine: An extremely toxic substance used as a pesticide

- Quinine: A chemical used as a pain reliever and anti-malaria drug

- Fentanyl: A powerful synthetic narcotic painkiller

Phenobarbital, caffeine, methaqualone and dirt have also been used to cut heroin. Along with these adulterants, an IV drug user may be injecting a whole host of impurities, not to mention bacterial and viral organisms. Do you really want to send all that garbage straight into the circulatory system that feeds your heart, lungs, and brain?

People who abuse heroin may develop infections of the heart valve and heart lining. This is extremely dangerous and requires medical attention. Because heroin causes shallow breathing and suppresses coughing, people who use heroin regularly are at risk of pneumonia and tuberculosis. Opiate drugs can suppress your immune system, making you more likely to catch colds and infections. Because heroin slows down your body's basic functions, it can also cause severe constipation. Hepatitis and HIV are extreme risks for those who shoot up heroin, as most users eventually do. Many times, heroin users are under the influence and do not take care to use clean needles, thus sharing them with others. Infections and collapsed veins are very common. If someone has HIV or Hepatitis C, whoever uses that needle next is susceptible to having the disease transmitted to them.

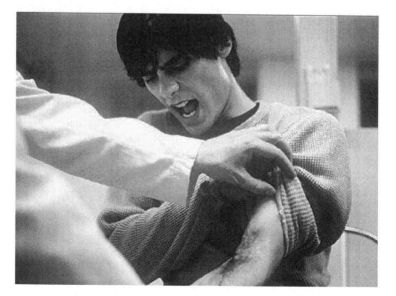

Besides the physical dangers associated with heroin addiction, there are many psychological and relational ones as well. Individuals hooked on heroin may become depressed, psychotic and paranoid. They may also ruin family relationships, destroy friendships and will likely find it hard to hold down a job. Many who are addicted and have children will lose custody of them because they are unable to care for them. Financial hardships often follow as all of the user's money is spent on drugs. Finally, legal consequences are generally found as heroin is an illegal drug, and the user may begin to get arrested for possession, sale or other related crimes.

Overdosing is a big risk with any illegal drug, but the potency of heroin and its direct effects on the central nervous system make it especially dangerous. Most IV drug users don't know the strength of the heroin they're taking, which means that there's no way to be sure how the drug will affect you. When you overdose on heroin, the central nervous system responds by:

- Slowing down your breathing

- Dropping your blood pressure

- Making you delirious

- Causing muscle spasms

- Making you unconscious or comatose

Overdose in the case of heroin and many other opiates is unique in that the drug itself slows down the brain signals that tell a person to keep breathing. Usually, when you fall asleep, your brainstem will automate the breathing process to continue moving your diaphragm up and down and move air through your lungs. Heroin blocks this automation so that when you fall asleep, you stop breathing. There are also what are commonly known as "near misses," where you fall asleep and almost don't wake up. It is scarily common. It is estimated that for every fatal overdose, there are an estimated 25 to 50 near misses.

Without immediate emergency medical treatment, a heroin overdose can lead to death. In 2014, the most recent year for which data are available, heroin overdose deaths surged by 28 percent to 10,500. Users who have overdosed on heroin may need respiratory support, intravenous fluids and emergency medication, such as Narcan, to counteract the effects of the narcotic.

Whether smoked, snorted or injected, heroin is highly addictive and will always lead to a buildup of tolerance, where increasingly larger amounts of the drug are required to achieve the same feeling. After awhile, the euphoric effect becomes elusive, and the addict has to continue to use mass quantities of the drug just to feel "normal." Heroin use has some elements and dangers to it that the painkillers do not. Every time a user does heroin, they are risking overdose and death on the levels way above those with prescription drugs. Whether the foray into heroin use was meant as a one-time experiment or a cross over from pain meds to save money and headache, many get much more than they bargained for with it. Heroin grabs hold quickly and refuses to let go.

There is a way out from heroin addiction and those who have found it will gladly tell you that it is much easier than the pains and fears that come with the day to day life of an IV drug addict. The first step is realizing that you need help and that you absolutely don't want to go on living this way any longer. No one can recover from something like this on their own. It simply can't be done. There is a ton of help available for the growing problem of heroin addiction, if you are ready, and know where to look. Be sure to check out the chapters on detox and then "A Way Out..." to get started.

New Opiates and Research Chemicals

Half the modern drugs could well be thrown out the window, except that the birds might eat them. – Martin Henry Fisher.

Drug addicts are nothing if not resourceful. Find something that produces desirable effects that may be somewhat difficult to access and they'll likely find a way. Aside from heroin, whose access levels may vary depending on geography, many opiates are an ongoing challenge for addicts. This is where we enter the realm of research chemicals. The aim of these experimental, synthetic, chemicals is to mimic the effects of popular drugs such as ecstasy, marijuana, and now opiates.

W-18

The research chemical called W-18 isn't new per se, but it's sure become popular in the past 18 months. First developed 30 years ago and discussed online in 2012, the chemical is a potent μ-opioid agonist that is believed to be up to 10,000x more potent than morphine and 100x stronger than Fentanyl. The drug is thought to be coming from Chinese labs, where research chemicals are mass-produced and then sold online in powder form. Dealers in the U.S. and Canada are manufacturing pills from W-18, that may or may not also contain Fentanyl, and the pills are being called "beans" or "shady 80s."

As if the infiltration of W-18 wasn't scary enough, many addicts have no idea what they're getting as W-18 is being cut with other drugs and passed off either as just Fentanyl or straight heroin. Also, the dealers who are pressing the pills locally can't create a consistent product, with some pills having much higher concentrations of the research chemical than others. Several batches of these drugs have been seized in the

U.S. and Canada in early 2016. In Alberta alone, where a lot W-18 has been found, Fentanyl fatalities nearly doubled in 2015.

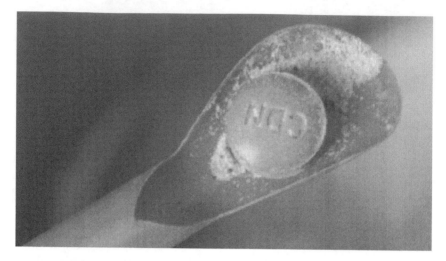

U-447700

Another deadly opiate-related research chemical is called U-447700. Originally patented by Upjohn in the 1970s, the chemical was shelved until being discovered by some enterprising chemist. Preliminary research showed that the drug is 7.5x more potent than morphine and addicts began purchasing the drug in powder form through online, unregulated sites. They have also been dying from its use. Deaths have been reported from U-447700 use in the U.S. and Europe, and it is now illegal in both Finland and Sweden.

Loperamide

While we often recommend Imodium as an over-the-counter (OTC) aid for opioid withdrawal, that isn't what we're talking about here. I remember being in one of many rehabs years ago and hearing about getting high from OTC medications. I went directly to the nearest drug store and filled up my shopping cart. I clearly wasn't ready to get clean. Opiate addicts that don't wish to give up their drugs are now turning to massive doses of Imodium A-D. The drug's main ingredient is reportedly a low-grade opioid agent that can produce a high. The

National Poison Center reports a 71 percent increase in Loperamide usage calls from 2011 to 2014. Large doses of this drug can be quite dangerous, leading to kidney and liver failure, heart issues, and even death.

Herbal Opiates

In every walk with Nature one receives far more than he seeks. — John Muir

While heroin itself is derived from the resin of the opium poppy plant, we have already devoted a section of the book to this drug. In this section, we're going to take a look at two different herbs, or drugs, which are also sought after by those who are looking for opiate-like effects. One is still readily available in most countries in stores and online, although not for human consumption. The other is also available online and in some stores, but not for the purposes that an opiate user would be using it for. Let's talk about Kratom and Poppy Tea.

Kratom

*This is how we bring about our own damnation,
you know - by ignoring the voice that begs us to
stop. To stop while there's still time. —Stephen
King, Revival*

Kratom, Mitragyna speciosa, is a tropical tree in the coffee family that is native to Southeast Asia, specifically indigenous to Thailand and Malaysia. Kratom leaves are often chewed fresh or dried out and made into tea or kratom capsules.

First described in an 1839 publication by Dutch botanist Pieter Willem Korthals, kratom has been used as a traditional medicine to reduce pain, as an anti-diarrheal, and as way of reducing opiate dependence. Of all the alkaloids present in the leaves, mitragynine appears to be the most active and the one most likely responsible for kratom's pleasing effects. Used as an opiate substitute, kratom contains no opiates of any kind, but it does bind to the same receptor sites in the brain. It binds to the mu-opioid receptor, as does morphine. Additionally mitragynine binds to kappa-opioid receptors, which are associated with pain relief and sedation. Mitragynine is adrenergic, which produces a stimulating effect, and it also binds with serotonin receptors, producing an anti-depressant effect as well. Due to this multiplicity of activities in the brain, kratom produces an overall pleasing feeling.

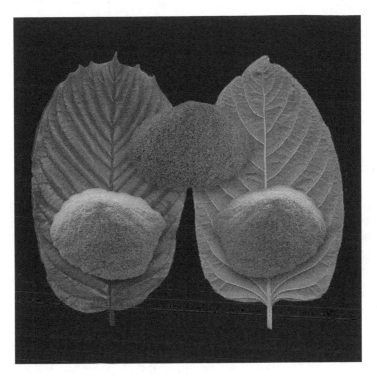

There is a lot about kratom that remains unknown. What is clear is that its use is becoming more widespread by those who are looking to manage chronic pain, without a prescription, and by those who are looking for an opiate substitute to use for the management of withdrawal. While successful use has been reported by users, in both circumstances, what is important to point out is the fact that kratom still produces opiate-like effects.

While kratom may not have significant adverse effects for those who use it recreationally, for the management of pain or for detox, the fact remains that it is a mood altering substance, and anyone susceptible to addiction is likely to turn to the chronic use of something that makes them feel good. In Southern Thailand, upwards of 70% of the male population uses kratom on a daily basis. How could this not be considered a "habit"? In fact, compulsive use of kratom has been reported, outside of Southeast Asia. The side effects associated with chronic kratom use include loss of appetite, weight loss, constipation, insomnia, dry mouth, and darkening of the skin.

Case in point is a medical case study [June 2008 Journal of Addiction] on a 43-year old male patient that became addicted to hydromorphone, using 10mg per day from crushed pills. He elected to manage his own opioid withdrawal at home with the use of kratom, which he purchased online. He made kratom tea four times per day, stating that it helped avert withdrawal symptoms and also helped him to feel "more alert." He subsequently spent over $15,000 per year on kratom. This other use wasn't for detox any longer. He had simply traded in one addiction for another.

Because kratom does modify mood, many agencies have taken notice, and kratom is on a DEA "watch list" for possible future regulation. So far, Indiana, Tennessee, and Vermont are the only states to ban the botanical on a state level although the DEA, in conjunction with the FDA, has shut down several US-based online kratom websites since the last half of 2014. Kratom is also banned in Australia, Myanmar, and Malaysia and is tightly restricted in many parts of Europe.

Despite being indigenous to Thailand and growing throughout the country, it has been banned there for over 70 years. What's most interesting is WHY kratom was banned in Thailand in the first place. You see, 70 years ago, much of the population there was hooked on opium and the government actually profited off of this by raking in "opium taxes." Kratom was being used to kick opium addiction, and the government didn't like the hit that their tax revenues were taking as a result - thus the ban. This ban is now looking at being lifted in the hopes that kratom can help with a rising meth addiction problem in the country.

So, what is the bottom line when it comes to kratom? I'm not sure, really. I think that it does have some real medicinal uses for the management of chronic pain, anxiety, and other issues. However, this is a book about opiate addiction and anything that produces opiate-like effects is going to be ripe for abuse, particularly for someone who is susceptible to addiction. This is the key thing to keep in mind with regards to any herb or ethnobotanical, regardless of the motivation for beginning its use.

Poppy Tea

There were opium-dens, where one could buy oblivion, dens of horror where the memory of old sins could be destroyed by the madness of sins that were new. — *Oscar Wilde*

Poppy tea is only marginally known about in opiate circles and not quite as easy to come by as in recent years. It is considered to be any herbally infused tea that is brewed from dried poppy straw or poppy seeds. Both the dried pods and seeds can be found through various sources online, but not for these purposes. Dried poppy pods are available for purchase as ornamental dried plants, not for human consumption. Poppy seeds are available in limited quantities for baking purposes - bagels, muffins, etc.

Poppy tea is not a new concoction at all. In fact, it is depicted in both Asian art and Western literature. Over 200 years ago, German chemist/pharmacist Friedrich Wilhelm Serturner discovered one of the key dangers of opium extracts, which is exactly what poppy tea is. Serturner indicated that, while opium extract was a superb analgesic, the dose could not be controlled well. Morphine and other opiates have what is known as a narrow therapeutic index - this is a very small range between the therapeutic effects of the drug and its toxic effects.

Poppy tea itself contains certain alkaloids from the plant, including morphine, codeine, papaverine, and thebaine. The effects of poppy tea vary depending on the amount ingested and are similar to any other opiate high. However, the danger is not knowing exactly what you are getting with each concoction. This is because the morphine content can vary by as much as 125 times (from 2 to 251 ug/g) depending upon the types of poppy straw, when they were harvested, or condition of poppy seeds. Poppy seeds themselves don't contain opiates but do have residual amounts on them from the pods. The numbers vary widely depending on well they are washed, if at all, before packaging and sale.

Another issue of concern with poppy tea is that many who use it are unaware of its action and half-life. When the tea is consumed, effects aren't usually felt until about 30 minutes later. Those not knowing this are at risk of drinking even more as the alkaloids build up in their system. Effects from poppy tea can last up to 12 hours, and the half-life of this substance can be incredibly long. Some users have reported withdrawal symptoms initiating over a month after the last dosage. What is rarely disputed is that poppy tea is just as addictive as any other opiate, and potentially much more dangerous.

As users increase their dosage of poppy tea, side effects generally ensue and these include drowsiness, stomach pain, lethargy, constipation, urinary retention, and nausea. At very high doses, respiratory arrest and death does occur. There have been quite a few reported deaths from poppy tea and several that have made local media headlines. In 2004, a California teen was using over 3 lbs of poppy seeds to produce poppy tea daily with the knowledge of his parents, although they were unaware of its dangers. He died with over five times the lethal opioid oral dose in his system. In 2009, 20-year-old University of Colorado student Alexander McGuiggan also died from a lethal dose of poppy tea, made from plants acquired online. In early 2016, a James Madison University (Virginia) student ingested a fatal dose of poppy tea. These are just a few cases of the overdoses and deaths that continue to pile up from this homemade concoction.

Addiction is common with those who use poppy tea, and this isn't an easy opiate to get away from. Because of its long half-life, the withdrawal is longer and more severe than with some other opiates. Withdrawal symptoms include muscle cramps, vomiting, diarrhea, headache, insomnia, lethargy, and anxiety. Psychological dependence can last much longer than the physical withdrawal, which could fade within ten days. Craving could go on for up to a year and additional treatment, as with other opiates is recommended. If treatment isn't pursued, recovery from this addiction is very difficult and many addicts either return to using poppy tea or graduate to the easier to obtain street drug - heroin.

If you are addicted to poppy tea, you are definitely not alone. Many people have unwittingly tried this powerful brew, having no idea what they were getting into and have wound up hopelessly addicted. Regardless, there is always hope. Please check out the chapters on opiate detox and treatment alternatives, as well as the section on the importance of a support group in recovery. As the ingredients for poppy tea have become harder and harder to come by, the frustration and terror of being addicted to this substance are sure to mount for those in its grip. Recovery is always possible and much simpler than this daily struggle.

Opiate Maintenance Drugs and Opiate Substitution Therapy

Be miserable. Or motivate yourself. Whatever has to be done, it's always your choice. -Wayne Dyer

Many people in the grip of opiate addiction simply can't imagine a life without opiates in them. It seems a complete impossibility. I was absolutely at this place at one point in time. I was taking so much of this stuff on a daily basis just to function and avoid getting sick that I couldn't imagine being able to lift up my head, much less handle living life, without some form of it. The thought of detox and withdrawal symptoms setting in was also a terrifying prospect and something to be avoided at all costs. I was convinced that this was something that would either land me in the emergency room or simply kill me, neither of which I could afford. Facing all of this, Opiate Replacement Therapy (ORT), or opiate substitution therapy, seemed the only answer. Some of these choices are available for long-term use as opiate maintenance drugs, others are available for short term use to assist in opiate detox, while others are recommended for short-term use yet used for maintenance purposes anyway. There are benefits and dangers to each one and, as is the case with any opiate derivative, each is also subject to some form of abuse.

Opiate substitution therapy itself is the process of replacing the abused opiate, such as heroin or pain pills, with a longer acting and less euphoric opioid. This would be something like Methadone or Suboxone, which is taken under medical supervision. The main idea behind ORT is that the opiate addict would be able to regain a normal life while being treated with a substance that prevents them from experiencing withdrawal symptoms and drug cravings, but doesn't provide the high or euphoria effect.

Methadone, Buprenorphine (Suboxone), and Naltrexone have all been approved by the FDA for the treatment of opiate addiction. There are also some recent breakthroughs with the drug Naloxone that are worth noting. Some of these drugs have been used longer than others and for different purposes. A few also have some very real dangers to be aware of before making the decision jump into any sort of ORT that could put you in a worse long-term position than you're in now. It may not seem that there are many choices available to you, but there are a few, and they should be considered carefully.

Methadone Programs and Methadone Addiction Dangers

Courage is the price that life exacts for granting peace. -Amelia Earhart

Methadone, also known as Symoron, Dolophine, Amidone, Methadose, Physeptone, and Heptadon among others, is a synthetic opioid that was developed in Germany in 1937. Methadone is a synthetic mu opioid receptor agonist and is administered orally in liquid, tablet, or dispersible tablet formulation. Methadone's ability to relieve the opiate withdrawal syndrome was noted as early as 1947 when it was introduced in the U.S. by Eli Lilly and Company, and within two years it became the preferred medication for detoxification at the national narcotics hospital in Lexington, Kentucky. It was not until 1964 when scientists at the Rockefeller Medical Research Institute (now University) began to evaluate methadone maintenance as a means of long-term medication-assisted treatment for opiate addiction. This work helped establish that not only did methadone relieve opiate withdrawal but, when at steady-state, it also blocked the euphoric and sedating effects of short-acting opiates taken on top of it.

Methadone is an opioid analgesic that is primarily a mu-opioid agonist. It has actions and uses similar to those of morphine. It also has a depressant action on the cough center and may be given to control an intractable cough associated with terminal lung cancer. Methadone is also used as part of the treatment of dependence on opioid drugs, although prolonged use of methadone itself may result in dependence. Methadone is also increasingly being prescribed by doctors as a pain medication, which has opened up wide channels of abuse by users searching for a cheap and easy way to get high. With methadone, however, the dangers are great and users often get much more than they bargained for.

The reasons that methadone is so very dangerous are several. One is that the drug has a very long half-life. This means that it takes a long time for a dose of methadone to metabolize through your system - sometimes days. When the user adds another dose to their system, the old one (and the one before that) are still in there processing, creating a toxic opiate pyramid of destruction. Another reason that methadone is deadly for many is its side effects and interactions with other drugs. Methadone can severely depress the respiratory system. Add this effect to other drugs that do the same, such as alcohol, other opiates, or Benzos, and you have a very deadly combination indeed.

Clearly, one of the most glaring problems with Methadone is the potential for overdose. Like other opiates, methadone users can develop a tolerance to the drug and, consequently, need higher and higher doses of it to achieve the same results. Often, this results in them seeking the drug outside of a controlled medical facility if this is where they were obtaining it originally. Currently, there are twice as many deaths attributed to methadone as to heroin. Some users will even begin selling their methadone and just return to street drugs.

One former addict, Billy, who has now been in a recovery program for four months, said he was on methadone for 21 years and during that time he was still using illegal drugs like heroin. He added: "I used to go and pick up 600ml or maybe more and it would go in the fridge unsupervised. And then I would go and sell my methadone, and I would go and buy heroin with it. Sometimes I had row after row of bottles, saving it up. I used to save it up and sell it." Billy said it was only when he enrolled in a residential recovery program, that he was able to start getting his life back to normal.

In the last decade, methadone has seen a surge in popularity as an attractive option for pain management. As a long-acting opiate with little to no euphoric effects, it was thought to be ideal. Less than a dollar a dose, the drug was three to four times cheaper than its closest competitor and 12 times cheaper than OxyContin. From 1999 to 2005, the use of methadone in the U.S. went from 965,000 grams to 5.4 million grams, according to the DEA. A drawback, however, is that unlike OxyContin, methadone is not technologically engineered for sustained release of the drug so blood concentrations will fluctuate greatly between dosing. Because of its properties and potential side effects, methadone taken for chronic pain must be taken properly and with due care. "This is a wonderful medicine used appropriately, but an unforgiving medicine used inappropriately," said Dr. Howard A. Heit, a pain specialist at Georgetown University. "Many legitimate patients, following the direction of the doctor, have run into trouble with methadone, including death."

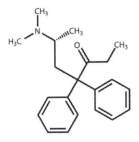

Methadone has recently come under scrutiny in the death of former Playboy model Anna Nicole Smith. A doctor in Studio City prescribed methadone to Smith for pain treatment before she was found dead in her Hollywood, FL., hotel suite. The doctor treating her said his treatment was "medically sound and appropriate." Months earlier,

Smith's 20-year-old son died in the Bahamas after taking a lethal mixture of methadone and two antidepressants, Zoloft and Lexapro.

So, does Methadone have no use whatsoever? Opinion varies. Some people are able to stay on it long-term and do well. I actually went on Methadone for about six weeks while I was on a waiting list to get into a treatment center. I couldn't continue to do what I was doing because I was breaking the law to get my drugs every day and couldn't risk it anymore. I also couldn't stay clean. I saw no other alternative. I can say that Methadone did keep the withdrawal symptoms and cravings at bay for the time that I took it so it served its purpose. However, I did go off of it cold turkey and that was very unpleasant. This isn't recommended and there are things to consider when you detox from methadone as methadone withdrawal can be very severe due to the buildup of the drug in your system. This is something to consider carefully either before you start taking the drug or when considering coming off of it. Check out the chapter on that here.

Suboxone and Buprenorphine - Miracle or Mess?

When we are no longer able to change a situation - we are challenged to change ourselves. -Viktor E. Frankl

Buprenorphine is a semi-synthetic opioid that is used to treat opioid addiction in higher dosages (>2 mg), to control moderate acute pain in non-opioid-tolerant individuals in lower dosages, and to control moderate chronic pain. It is available in a variety of formulations: Subutex, Suboxone (Buprenorphine HCl and naloxone HCl; typically used for opioid addiction), Temgesic (sublingual tablets for moderate to severe pain), Buprenex (solutions for injection often used for acute pain in primary care settings), Norspan and Butrans (transdermal preparations used for chronic pain). Buprenorphine was first marketed in the 1980's as an analgesic and in 2002 the FDA approved Suboxone and Subutex for detox and replacement therapy in opioid dependency.

Suboxone is a partial opiate agonist, thus has a lower risk of overdose and addiction than methadone. It is a bit more difficult to abuse than methadone but is also less effective than methadone. As a partial opiate agonist, the Buprenorphine in Suboxone may provide a slight pleasurable sensation but many who take it simply say that they feel "normal" and are able to function. The drug tricks the brain into thinking that it has the full opioid agonist and thus prevents withdrawal symptoms from commencing.

The other ingredient of Naloxone is actually an opioid blocker which can trigger withdrawal symptoms should someone try to abuse the drug by crushing it, snorting it or injecting it. Suboxone is also supposed to have what is called a "ceiling effect." This means that taking more than prescribed will not result in a full opioid effect, flush with euphoric feelings. This also helps if Buprenorphine is taken in overdose levels as there is less of the suppressed breathing side effect than would be had with a full opiate agonist.

Suboxone is a long-acting opiate, with a 24 hours+ half-life, so it only needs to be taken once daily.   In September 2012, Reckitt Benckiser Pharmaceuticals, one of the manufacturers of Suboxone, voluntarily withdrew their tablet formulation of the drug from the market due to the much higher number of child poisonings with that form of the drug.   These were replaced with dissolvable films.   Regardless, just a few short months later, the patent ran out on the drug and in February 2013, the FDA approved generic formulations of Buprenorphine tablets. So, back on the market they came.

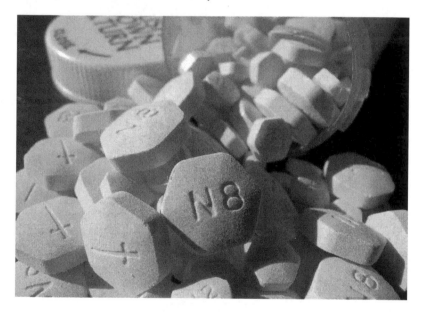

Aside from the danger to children (which is serious), it sounds as if this drug is a godsend and abuse proof, right? Wrong. It absolutely can be abused, is abused, and I've done it myself. I personally took more than my share of Buprenorphine quite a few years ago, stockpiled it and don't recall any adverse effects. What I do recall is not suffering withdrawal symptoms from painkillers but essentially just switching my allegiance from one drug to another for a short period of time because it was being handed to me by an addiction doctor. I certainly craved more of the Buprenorphine and, had it been offered to me, would have downed it in a heartbeat.

Several studies have now examined the reinforcing effects and abuse potential of Buprenorphine. Research has demonstrated that Buprenorphine does exhibit positive-reinforcement properties, similar to other opioids, making it ripe for the picking. Buprenorphine abuse by injection was first recorded in the mid-1980s. In the last two-and-a-half decades, Buprenorphine diversion and illicit use have been documented in countries around the world, including the United States. In some countries, such as Finland, Buprenorphine is the most widely abused opioid.

Make no mistake - this is a very powerful drug. Buprenorphine is estimated to be 25 to 45 times as powerful as morphine. One of the treatment regimens approved by the FDA is for long term maintenance. Be very wary should someone, M.D. after their name or not, suggest this to you. Your brain chemistry absolutely cannot heal and regenerate as it needs to while continuing to take such a powerful narcotic on a daily basis. Long-term doses, even as low as 2mg, can block almost all of a person's emotions, and this has been reported time and again with Suboxone.

So, now sufficiently warned and probably turned off from the drug for good, here's how it can help you. Even some of the biggest opponents of this drug agree on the fact that Buprenorphine, and particularly Suboxone, makes an excellent drug for supervised opiate detox. Generally, this is best used in an inpatient treatment setting, but a closely monitored outpatient setting is possible as well. This involves using Suboxone in a tapering manner for a fixed period of time (days not weeks) in order to manage opiate detox and prevent the onset of withdrawal symptoms.

As was the case with OxyContin, Suboxone is widely promoted by doctors as being nonaddictive, but the experience of many addicts proves otherwise: Bupe, or Subs, can be harder to kick than methadone once addicted - and methadone is a beast to kick. At the high doses many physicians prescribe—8 to 24 mg— some say it's almost impossible to do without professional help. While many people may find an improvement in the quality of life as a result of getting off illicit drugs, they are still going to be suffering physically and emotionally from the effects of an opiate when they take Suboxone. The best answer is to experience life drug-free, and when that sobriety lasts the rest of one's life, that is even better.

Naltrexone Use and Its Effectiveness

If there is no struggle, there is no progress. -
Frederick Douglass

Naltrexone is an opioid receptor antagonist used primarily in the management of alcohol dependence and opioid dependence. It is marketed in generic form as its hydrochloride salt, naltrexone hydrochloride, and sold under the trade names Revia and Depade. In some countries, including the United States, a once-monthly extended-release injectable formulation is marketed under the trade name Vivitrol.

Naltrexone works by blocking the effects of opiates in the brain. Naltrexone is not a narcotic. As an opiate receptor agonist, it is able to block the reaction from the part of the brain that produces feelings of pleasure when opiates are taken. It has been shown to reduce drug cravings in some people but not all. It is also not effective as a detox drug to keep withdrawal symptoms from occurring. Naltrexone is not an opiate replacement drug per se. Its primary use is to help those who have already stopped using drugs to not return to them. Regardless, it is often used in maintenance programs and used long-term by some.

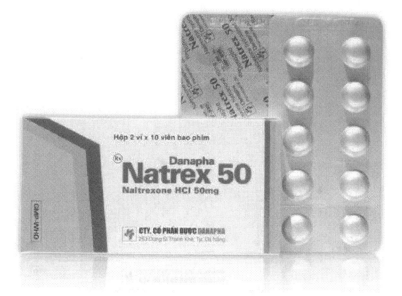

One thing to caution is that if you begin taking Naltrexone with opiates in your system, even coming off of a Suboxone detox, it will trigger withdrawal symptoms. The length of time between detoxing from opiates and beginning Naltrexone varies and should be physician-supervised as it greatly depends on the particular opiate and its half-life, the amount consumed, and your particular body chemistry.

Many people begin taking Naltrexone after some sort of detox regimen or treatment program and want to commit to remaining drug-free. For a lot of people, this is highly unnecessary if the proper support is in place and they are committed to a solid recovery program. However, should you wish to use Naltrexone, be sure that it is indicated for your situation. You must let your doctor know if:

- You have recently taken any opiate drugs

- If you have liver or kidney problems.

- If you are pregnant, trying to get pregnant, or are breastfeeding.

- If you are taking or using any other medicines. This includes any medicines you are taking which are available to buy without a prescription, such as herbal and complementary medicines.

- If you have ever had an allergic reaction to any medicine.

The most common side effects reported with naltrexone are non-specific gastrointestinal complaints such as diarrhea and abdominal cramping. There has been some controversy regarding the use of opioid-receptor antagonists, such as Naltrexone, in the long-term management of opioid dependence due to the effect of these agents in sensitizing the opioid receptors. That is, after therapy, the opioid receptors continue to have increased sensitivity for a period during which the patient is at increased risk of opioid overdose. This effect reinforces the necessity of monitoring of therapy and provision of patient support measures by medical practitioners. Weigh the benefits and risks carefully and make an informed decision about the maintenance use of Naltrexone.

Naloxone Uses and Recent Breakthrough Research

*When you reach the end of your rope, tie a knot
in it and hang on. -Thomas Jefferson*

Naloxone is an opioid inverse agonist drug developed by Sankyo in the 1960s. Naloxone has traditionally been a drug used to counter the effects of opiate overdose, for example, heroin or morphine overdose. Naloxone is specifically used to counteract life-threatening depression of the central nervous system and respiratory system. Naloxone is marketed under various trademarks including Narcan, Nalone, and Narcanti.

Naloxone is most commonly injected intravenously for fastest action, which usually causes the drug to act within a minute, and last up to 45 minutes. It can also be administered via intramuscular or subcutaneous injection. Naloxone has an extremely high affinity for μ-opioid receptors in the central nervous system, as it is designed to pluck out all opiates in its path in order to reverse an overdose. Naloxone is a μ-opioid receptor competitive antagonist, and its rapid blockade of those receptors often produces rapid onset of withdrawal symptoms. However, it is a temporary drug that wears off in 20-90 minutes.

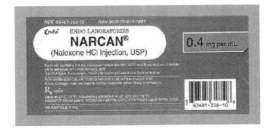

Paramedics in Clermont County, Ohio, twice saved the life of 19-year-old Mason Rue with Narcan. The Batavia man overdosed on heroin first as a Batavia High School sophomore and again as a senior. "I was told I'd been pronounced dead for 32 seconds," Rue said during an interview at a rehab, where he and his girlfriend, Samantha Gabriele, 21, a recovering painkiller addict, attend couple's therapy. Rue said he had injected a gram of heroin and taken Xanax - a prescription medication to treat anxiety disorder - and lost consciousness on his mother's couch. Rue said he woke up about 30 seconds after being injected to a blinding light. "My body felt numb. Then I felt electric static in my legs. I had indescribable cramps and threw up," Rue said. "I woke up to a living hell but am 100 percent glad I was brought back."

All of this being said, how can this be used in opiate maintenance therapy? Well, it really can't but its access for those who need it is expanding substantially and any opiate addict, recovered or not, will be glad to know it. You see, Naloxone is a non-toxic, non-narcotic, non-addictive drug. The potential for abuse is nil, but its ability to reverse a potentially fatal opioid overdose is great. The drug is currently unavailable without a prescription and, at times, there have even been shortages of it on the market. Most people in the midst of an overdose don't have time to make a doctor's appointment and drive to the local pharmacy.

In 2012, the FDA for the first time has advocated making Naloxone available without a prescription, although this hasn't happened yet. Also, the director of the National Institute on Drug Abuse, Dr. Nora Volkow, has said that the drug should be available without a prescription. In fact, Naloxone distribution, in the form of "heroin overdose kits" is already being piloted in some areas, such as San Francisco to great success. Anyone with a history of opiate abuse or who has loved ones in its grip would do well to have this on hand when it becomes available. In Australia, Naloxone is already available over the counter in most pharmacies.

Naloxone is being distributed and carried on hand in a steadily increasing number of jurisdictions in the just the past year. Police officers in Quincy, Massachusetts, Staten Island, NY, Ocean County, NJ and Espanola Valley, NM all now carry the nasal spray form of the drug. As of mid-2014, an additional 20,000 officers in New York began carrying Naloxone. The CDC estimates the US programs for drug users and their caregivers prescribing take-home doses of Naloxone and training on its use are estimated to have prevented 10,000 opioid overdose deaths.

There are also recent research breakthroughs in the potential for a "Heroin Vaccine" in the not too distant future. In May 2013, a study released by the Scripps Research Institute showed that a heroin-blocking vaccine is now ready for human trials. Senior study author Kim Janda says the vaccine causes the body to produce antibodies against heroin and its psychoactive products. These antibodies circulate in the bloodstream and neutralize any of these substances they encounter before they reach the brain. "It's like the old '80s game Pac-Man," Janda said. "They immediately seek out the target and sequester it." The vaccine isn't intended to provide a one-step solution for heroin addicts, Koob said. It's meant to help addicts who want to get off the drug, by eliminating the damaging effect of a relapse. Scripps investigators are currently seeking funding to begin human trials of the vaccine, possibly in the next year.

Opiate Addiction and the Disease Concept

It ain't what you don't know that gets you into trouble. It's what you know for sure that just ain't so. -Mark Twain

Few people in this world are not touched by addiction in some form. Whether suffering from it themselves, growing up in a household with an addicted family member or having a friend or loved one who is an addict, it is far-reaching. We all have our preconceived notions about addiction and many of them, unfortunately, are based on false information or misconceptions about addicts and addiction itself. Many people think of addicts as people who simply lack self-control, moral fiber or proper upbringing. For those of us that find ourselves in the grip of addiction, yet have these things (self-control, moral fiber, etc.) in other areas of our lives, this can be confusing and downright frustrating. What comes as a revelation to many, as well as a relief, is the knowledge that addiction is, in fact, a disease and not a moral issue. In other words, those suffering from addiction aren't bad people, they're sick people.

The American Medical Association (AMA) broke new ground approximately forty years ago when it declared alcoholism to be a disease. And in the past decade, dramatic advances in technology have allowed scientists to examine the brain itself in search of the causes, mechanisms, and consequences of addiction. Today, scientists and physicians overwhelmingly agree that while use and even abuse of drugs such as alcohol and cocaine is a behavior over which the individual exerts control, addiction to these substances is something entirely different. Scientists have begun to understand why addicted people may sacrifice everything that's important to them - their jobs, their families, their homes - in the quest for a chemical fix.

"When you get into an addicted state, it's a disease of the brain," says Alan Leshner, Ph.D., director of the federal government's National Institute on Drug Abuse (NIDA). Leshner says the stigma associated with alcohol and drug addiction is one of the biggest problems experts continually face in dealing with it. Leshner says that the public has little sympathy for addicts, but he adds that "whether you like the person or not, you've got to deal with [their problem] as an illness."

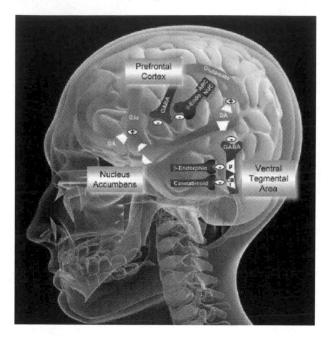

Addiction is considered a physiological disease because it meets the same requirements as other disorders and diseases, including a great deal of terminal illnesses. This is important to note because unabated addiction is 100% fatal. The basic requirements which clearly classify addiction as a disease include:

- The symptoms are the same across many different types of substances. For instance, whether your drug of choice is heroin or alcohol, the general symptoms are always the same

- Addiction is chronic and does not subside without treatment

- Addiction symptoms are progressive, resulting in death

- Just as other diseases surface repeatedly, addiction results in an extremely high occurrence of relapse

- Addiction and alcoholism are treatable

This doesn't, however, relieve the addict from any responsibility simply because they have been labeled as a "disease sufferer". Quite the contrary. Dr. Volkow of the NIDA explains, "People say if you consider drug addiction a disease, you are taking the responsibility away from the drug addict. But that's wrong. If we say a person has heart disease, are we eliminating their responsibility? No. We're having them exercise. We want them to eat less, stop smoking. The fact that we have a disease recognizes that there are changes, in this case, in the brain".

Addiction is typically diagnosed by a series of behaviors as opposed to physical symptoms or any type of medical testing. These behaviors can be summarized as repeated failure to control the substance abuse despite severe consequences. This means that an addict will lose control over a substance, obsess over it, and continue even when they know that there is imminent danger or risk of life-changing consequences.

Under the disease model of addiction, the brain's motivational center becomes reorganized. The priorities are shuffled so that finding and using the substance (or another substance that will produce similar effects) becomes top priority as far as the brain is concerned. In this sense, the drug has essentially taken over the brain, and the addict is no longer in control of his behavior. An alcoholic won't, for example, have trouble deciding whether or not to get in his car and drive to the store to get more alcohol - the urge will be irresistible.

The disease of addiction has a target organ known as the mid brain. The cause is regulatory dysfunction of a neurotransmitter called dopamine. The effect is a common group of symptoms seen in each and every alcoholic and addict known to have the disease of dependence: loss of control, craving, and persistent use despite adverse consequences. Many alcoholics and addicts have been accused of selfishness, of choosing their behaviors for a reward or pleasure, since that portion of the brain targeted by drugs has often been called the reward or pleasure center. This impression of hedonistic behavior on the part of the addict has for a long time caused inappropriate judgment, bringing shame to the one who suffers from this disease.

Long-term abuse causes changes in other brain chemical systems and circuits as well. Glutamate is a neurotransmitter that influences the reward circuit and the ability to learn. When the optimal concentration of glutamate is altered by drug abuse, the brain attempts to compensate, which can impair cognitive function. Brain imaging studies of drug-addicted individuals show changes in areas of the brain that are critical to judgment, decision-making, learning and memory, and behavior control. Together, these changes can drive a substance abuser to seek out and take drugs compulsively despite adverse, even devastating, consequences— that is the nature of addiction.

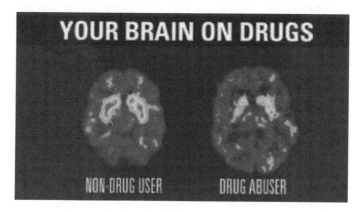

No single factor can predict whether a person will become addicted to drugs. Risk for addiction is influenced by a combination of factors that include individual biology, social environment, and age or stage of development. The more risk factors an individual has, the greater the chance that taking drugs can lead to addiction. For example:

- **Biology**. The genes that people are born with —in combination with environmental influences —account for about half of their addiction vulnerability. Additionally, gender, ethnicity, and the presence of other mental disorders may influence risk for drug abuse and addiction.

- **Environment.** A person's environment includes many different influences, from family and friends to socioeconomic status and quality of life in general. Factors such as peer pressure, physical and sexual abuse, stress, and quality of parenting can greatly influence the occurrence of drug abuse and the escalation to addiction in a person's life.

- **Development.** Genetic and environmental factors interact with critical developmental stages in a person's life to affect addiction vulnerability. Although taking drugs at any age can lead to addiction, the earlier that drug use begins, the more likely it will progress to more serious abuse, which poses a special challenge to adolescents. Because areas in their brains that govern decision making, judgment, and self-control are still developing, adolescents may be especially prone to risk-taking behaviors, including trying drugs of abuse.

It is not an issue of free will or behavioral control; addiction is a physical, neurological disease for which there is no known cure – only treatment to manage it. Just as a person wouldn't treat a terminal illness at home, an addict or alcoholic should be able to expect to get help at a professional facility just as they would with any disease. The most difficult part of the disease of addiction is that an addict will almost never get help on their own because the very nature of the illness will not allow the sufferer to believe they are afflicted by it. Often before becoming willing to ask for help, it is necessary to come to the realization that you are not "bad," just sick. Once this sinks in, the idea that there is a way out can begin to take form.

You never find yourself until you face the truth. -Pearl Bailey

A Way Out for the Opiate Addict

If we don't change our direction, we are likely to end up where we are headed. -Ancient Chinese Proverb

Being addicted to opiates is maddening. I spent many years in this endless cycle of fear, loss and pain. When in the depths of an addiction, it seems as if there is no way out and as if no one could possibly understand how you feel. Life without a drug that was needed to simply allow me to function on a daily basis seemed an impossibility yet the life that I was living was getting infinitely worse, and it was clear that I was either going to end up losing my freedom or my life. When my addiction started, I was in my early 20s, had a pretty great life and few worries in the world. Towards the end, I was 30, in poor health, depressed, and on the verge of losing everything.

Despite this pretty picture, make no mistake about it - There absolutely IS a way out for the opiate addict or any addict for that matter. This is a recovery process so, unfortunately, no magic pill can be taken where you wake up tomorrow white as snow as if this nightmare never happened. And, before this process can even begin, it must be proceeded by some pain, suffering and soul-searching. This usually isn't too tall of an order, and most addicts have seen a good deal of this already. The question is - was it enough?

I was first arrested for prescription fraud in my mid-20s, when doctor shopping just wasn't providing me with enough pills to satisfy my need anymore. It was at this point that the criminal justice system entered my life, and remained there for many years to come. I also began getting sent to treatment centers by the courts, who in turn, pushed me into 12 step recovery rooms. I can tell you that I was absolutely indignant and appalled that anyone would suggest that I had a "problem." Despite the fact that I kept committing the same crimes over and over again and was incapable of staying clean for even one day, I did not want help nor was I willing to listen to the experiences and advice of others. It took several more years, a lot more losses, and finding my "bottom" to make any sort of a beginning in recovery. It doesn't need to be this difficult.

The best way out is always through. —*Robert Frost*

Why Hitting Bottom is a Must

When you're drowning, you don't say 'I would
be incredibly pleased if someone would have the
foresight to notice me drowning and come and
help me,' you just scream. -John Lennon

Who hasn't heard the phrase "hitting rock bottom" before? It takes on new meaning, however, when it comes to addiction and when you're the one hitting it.   One thing is for certain; no one else can define your bottom for you. As much as family members, judges and counselors would love to take on this role, it is up to the individual alone to decide when enough is enough, and it's time to make a change. There is, in fact, some controversy, over the notion that addicts must hit bottom in order to recover. I think that this is hogwash and just playing with semantics. The fact of the matter is that until such time as the way we are living becomes painful, uncomfortable and unmanageable enough, we are not going to be willing to make any changes, and that includes the frightening notion of asking for help.

Reaching a bottom, however, can be vastly different for everyone. For some, it could be the loss of "things", status, or relationships. For others, it is more of an emotional state where they simply can't stand the way they feel inside anymore. One person could lose their car or their job and be sufficiently effected to cry "mercy" and get help. Still another could go from Park Ave to the homeless shelter in a very short time and see nothing amiss, or at least not see that it is the drug use that is at the root of their problems. Someone else may still have their home, their job, their marriage and their children yet feel very alone, ashamed and hopeless to the point that they cry out for help.

Others have a series of bottoms, where they swear they are "done", yet are able to justify continued use until more things continue to slip out of their lives. This is how it was for me. I started out as a highly educated professional with a home, good friends, and an adorable small child. In the end, I had lost many of my possessions, jobs, and friends. I was also losing custody of my son and looking at going to prison for five years - all over opiates. I've heard about "bottoms" that you've hit your bottom when that thing you've just lost or about to lose is more important to you than that next drink or drug. This was absolutely true for me. The prospect of losing my child and my freedom was enough to snap my head up and raise the white flag.

Addiction changes your life in so many ways. You can often find yourself saying or doing things that you would never have considered doing before you developed an addiction. You may have sworn that you would never cheat or steal, but suddenly find yourself doing these sorts of things in order to get your drug of choice. The important thing to realize is that your bottom does not need to look or feel like anyone else's. You don't need to sink to a certain deep dark place, be homeless, get arrested, or lose your job to be done. In fact, the simple fear of these things and the understanding that they ARE around the corner for you should you continue to use (we call these "Yets") is sufficient for many to make their beginning. Another thing to consider is that we often don't reach our bottom alone and, sometimes, can be prevented from reaching our bottom by well-meaning others.

Many addicts are so lost in their addictions and become so self-centered that they don't see what they are doing to family and loved ones. These people frequently watch in disbelief as the addict continues to use while life falls apart around them. This is painful and very hurtful. Well-meaning family members will sometimes step away from the situation and wait for the "bottom" to come or, worse yet, enable the addict by preventing consequences of using from occurring through financial assistance or otherwise. Hint: addicts don't seek help when things are going good or even when life is status quo.

I'm not suggesting at all that anyone make life more difficult for the addict. They will easily and quite quickly do this on their own. However, if someone you love is suffering from this disease, the best course of action is to stop enabling them and to educate them as much as possible about their disease and the recovery process. By cutting off money, shelter, legal support or emotional support, family members often can "raise the bottom" for the addict and perhaps help them find that place of unmanageability sooner rather than later. Through intervention and education, information about addiction is being passed on with kindness and compassion. Many addicts simply don't know that help is out there, or the information has not been presented to them in the proper manner.

Addiction is a cunning, baffling, and powerful disease. We've all heard of "denial" and this plays a huge part in hitting bottom and being ready to get help. The disease of addiction is the only illness people can experience and yet remain oblivious, in fact indignant, to the fact that they have a serious ailment that needs immediate attention. Simple logic says if you break your arm, you have a problem which will require immediate attention; the body and mind work together to make it quite obvious to you that the limb will not work properly until it is treated. Addiction, on the other hand, works in just the opposite way; even as the physical symptoms begin to manifest themselves, the disease sabotages the message between body and mind in order to keep the addict captive to the whims of the illness.

So where is your bottom? It depends on several factors. First and foremost, the realization and acceptance that there is an addiction and everything that comes along with it is a start. Second, is the understanding that things will continue to get worse should you continue to use. A common saying is that addiction ends in "jails, institutions, and death". This is absolutely true and is the case with untreated addiction. Third, is the notion that you can get off the elevator at any time, i.e., - stop going down further. Recovery from addiction is more than just possible; it is happening all around us on a daily basis. All it takes is a beginning, and each one of us is capable of deciding for ourselves when enough is enough, when to stop fighting, and when to try something else.

At fifteen life had taught me undeniably that surrender, in its place, was as honorable as resistance, especially if one had no choice. -Maya Angelou

Family and Loved Ones of the Addict

Addicts don't deny that they're using. They deny that it's hurting others. - Bob Poznanovich

Many family members know for a fact that there is an addiction issue while some continue to wish it away or look for any reassurance from the family member in question that things are "ok." Hint: addicts are masters at giving these sorts of reassurances and guarantees, even if they have no idea that they're doing so at the time. So, in order to get rid of the ambiguity, here is a list of questions, from the National Institute on Drug Abuse (NIDA), that you can ask yourself with regards to your loved one:

1. Does the person take the drug in larger amounts or for longer than they meant to?

2. Do they want to cut down or stop using the drug but can't?

3. Do they spend a lot of time getting, using, or recovering from the drug?

4. Do they have cravings and urges to use the drug?

5. Are they unable to manage their responsibilities at work, home, or school, because of drug use?

6. Do they continue to use a drug, even when it causes problems in their relationships?

7. Do they give up important social, recreational or work-related activities because of drug use?

8. Do they use drugs again and again, even when it puts them in danger?

9. Do they continue to use, even when they know they have a physical or psychological problem that could have been caused or made worse by the drug?

10. Do they take more of the drug to get the effect they want?

11. Have they developed withdrawal symptoms, which can be relieved by taking more of the drug? (Some withdrawal symptoms can be obvious, but others can be more subtle—like irritability or nervousness.)

If the answer to just a few of those questions was "yes", there is serious concern about addiction. Now, even in cases of iatrogenic, or "accidental" addiction, the answers to quite a few of these questions would still be affirmative. The addict may wish to cut down and find that they cannot, may have difficulty managing some responsibilities, may continue to use the drugs despite symptoms worsening due to their effects, and could be experiencing withdrawal symptoms for a variety of reasons. Drugs that originate in a doctor's office or pharmacy make them no less lethal and when an addict is your spouse, child, or parent, determining the course of action can take an added sense of urgency. Fault doesn't come into this and needs to be taken off of the table entirely if you expect to gain the trust of your loved one.

With regards to heroin addiction, the signs may be much more subtle. Physical indicators of heroin use include the presence of such things as pipes, aluminum foil, baggies, and syringes. Behaviors such as loss of appetite, drowsiness, muscle cramps, restlessness, and unpredictability are signs of drug use. Other signs include lying and secretiveness, missing valuables in the home, and legal issues.

If they want help and wish to get off of opiates, this is great. The best thing to do is to support them on this long road ahead. You may need to help them find a physician who can help with a withdrawal program or, better yet, an inpatient treatment center. There are areas of support that we talk about in the sections of this book on withdrawing from drugs at home. Finally, a source of moral support is one of the most important things that someone in recovery needs.

If your loved one does not recognize that there is a problem or if your concerns are met with anger and denial, there is still hope. Responding with anger usually won't get you very far, but it's important for the person addicted to understand that their behavior is no longer healthy and that you don't wish to watch them come to further harm or, even worse, die. If all else fails, an intervention may be helpful in getting them to see the negative effects that drugs have had on their lives and those around them. This is a carefully planned process that involves family and friends of the addicted person, who confront them as a group. This is not done to embarrass them but to get their attention and to get a very important message across. Whether you involve a professional interventionist, counselor or addiction specialist will be up to you. This idea is to give your loved one an opportunity to change directions and make some healthy changes with some clear support.

If all else fails, there are now quite a few states that have passed laws allowing for involuntary addiction treatment. This means that, should you be really determined and have a physician's backing, you can petition a judge to force your loved one into treatment. I would only recommend this under the most extreme situations, possibly where opiates are being abused severely, making each day of continued use a life threatening situation.

It often seems like those closest to addicts are the ones that suffer the most. I have been the addict that has inflicted the suffering on others, and I have been the loved one that has suffered. Neither is a walk in the park, and I have much sympathy for both sides. What I have learned through these experiences is that nothing helps to keep an addict sick more than enabling. Once my family members stopped doing this for me, I got better. Therefore, I do my best not to do it for anyone else. This can be a tough, but important, undertaking when you see someone that you love suffering. For more help on these sorts of issues, check out the family support groups in the Resources Section.

The Recovery Process Explained

Asking for help does not mean that we are weak or incompetent. It usually indicates an advanced level of honesty and intelligence. -Jim Rohn

When the addict finally hits some sort of bottom, "cries uncle" and decides to get some help, the recovery process can begin. Addicts love to live, suffer and try to take care of things in isolation. This is not, however, how recovery from addiction works. Getting away and staying away from drugs is not something that can be accomplished alone. Even if you decide to go through detox at home and forgo going to treatment, there is still no possible way to recover from opiate addiction on your own. A sick mind cannot cure a sick mind - plain and simple. Recovery requires making drastic changes in one's life and one's attitudes, and this cannot be done with self-help books, internet forums, Facebook, or wishful thinking. Hence the requirement for "hitting bottom". This requires taking actions that those who aren't sufficiently motivated wouldn't be willing to take.

First things first - when we think of getting off of drugs, the idea of actually getting off of drugs is terrifying. Detox from opiates is no cakewalk, and we have likely been scrambling on a daily basis for quite some time to avoid any sort of withdrawal symptoms from setting in. To think that we would now willingly allow this to happen seems madness. However, at many points in this process, it's important to remember why you're doing this. One thing you may wish to do, for easy access, is write it down. List out the reasons why you are stopping and the negative consequences that you have experienced as a result of your addiction. Write down the sorts of things you wish to gain and the kind of life that you want to have by getting clean. This list is for your benefit only but keep it close at hand for those reminders when needed.

You will also need to plan your detox and recovery. For some, this takes all of two minutes where they finally scream for help, and a loved one throws them in the car for a long prayed-for trip to the local rehab center. For others, options are weighed, and work and family arrangements are made. There are several opiate detox alternatives, and these are covered in the next section of the book. Detox is NOT the same as treatment, and treatment is NOT the same as a support group.

One of my first mistakes, and biggest eye openers occurred years ago when I first realized that I was hooked on painkillers and was not going to be able to stop taking them without getting sick. I honestly thought that I had only a physical dependence and, once through a quick detox, would be able to re-start my life with a clean slate. I took one day off of work, scheduled a rapid detox at a local hospital for a Friday-Sunday and planned to check out of the hospital and go right back to work on Monday morning, clean as a whistle. I did check out of the hospital on Monday morning, finished with the detox, and was using again by lunchtime. I was completely floored and devastated. I had had no idea what a grip this thing had on me until that time. I actually just gave into it and used for several more years before getting clean.

In order to recover from this disease, an entire program of recovery must be incorporated into one's life and it must take priority. This starts with detox, is often followed by a treatment program (though this is not always necessary) and is supplemented by participation in a recovery support group (absolutely necessary), preferably with emphasis on the 12 steps. The only way to stay clean from opiates long term is to change the addict and the only way to do this is through participation in one of these programs. But to get clean, you need to stop using.

Managing Opiate Detox and Detox from Opiates Alternatives

Your present circumstances don't determine where you can go; they merely determine where you start. -Nido Qubein

It is estimated that nearly 75% of addicts who check themselves into detox are there for some sort of opiate detox. Many addicts continue to use for years, not because the drug is providing them with the high that they enjoyed in the beginning, but because they are terrified of experiencing withdrawal symptoms that are sure to set in should they quit. During the course of their addiction, opiate addicts change the chemical makeup of their bodies. When the drugs are no longer available, alarm bells in the brain and nervous system begin to sound, and a variety of withdrawal symptoms start to manifest themselves. Opiate withdrawal symptoms may include:

- Abdominal pain

- Nausea

- Vomiting and diarrhea

- Insomnia

- Sweating

- Muscle aches

- Anxiety and agitation

While opiate withdrawal is generally not life threatening, it can be very uncomfortable and can last for up to a week. Psychologically this can be difficult to bear as cravings set in immediately, and the addict knows that symptoms can be alleviated simply by returning to using. This is why, many times, it is best to find some sort of structured detox program that provides a level of comfort and security. If the opiate addict is comfortable at least, they are more likely to complete the detox process and move on to the next step.

Is this always the case? Not necessarily, no. It can be argued that we often make it too easy and too comfortable for the addict to detox from drugs and, hence, there are no consequences and little motivation to stay clean. I understand this completely and can point to my first experience with rapid detox, where I walked out of the hospital and used again immediately. Rehabs have also provided me with medical detox in the past that was slow and steady, and not much appreciated. I have also detoxed from opiates on my own, the last time, and it's something that I am not likely to ever forget.

Also, consider that you will need to break ties with your suppliers BEFORE starting this process. Every good drug addict has a supplier and back-up, or ten. Don't wait until after you go through detox to deal with this. How were you obtaining your drugs on a regular basis and what is your plan of action with regards to that source(s) in the future? This could very well be the family doctor or a pain management doctor if you are addicted to pain meds. If you obtained your drugs illegally, consider that you are going to have to break ties with these contacts. You will need to delete them from your phone, block the numbers, do whatever you need to do. The temptations and cravings will be very strong at times, and this is one of the reasons why some self-examination is essential before starting the recovery process. Know why you are doing this and be fully committed. Don't give yourself a bunch of "outs" and escape routes if you want to be successful.

The success of your opiate detox has just as much to do with your "bottom" as anything else. If you are truly done using and ready to recover, simply get through the detox however you need to and move forward from there. That being said, there are several options to get you through opiate withdrawal including:

- Rapid Opiate Detox

- Ibogaine Treatment

- Medical Opiate Detox

- Opiate Detox at Home

There are also special considerations for detoxing from methadone (and suboxone) as these are very long-acting opiates. We'll also talk about the possibility of tapering and some tips on managing cravings as this important information whether you are just getting started or currently in recovery from opiate addiction.

Rapid Opiate Detox - The Facts and Risks

If you're going through hell, keep going. -
Winston Churchill

Rapid Opiate Detox (ROD), and sometimes also called Ultra Rapid Detox (UROD), is the process by which the withdrawal process is condensed into a very short period of time, anywhere from hours to a few days. The patient may be placed under anesthesia or simply lightly sedated while infused with a multitude of drugs, such as Naltrexone, to accelerate the detoxification process. The idea is to rush the withdrawal while you are "asleep" and to speed up the return to normal opioid system functioning.

Sounds ideal, doesn't it? Who wouldn't want the gain without the pain? Well, most addicts actually. Unfortunately, results aren't quite as advertised - it's incredibly expensive, and it's quite dangerous. The average cost for this is anywhere from $4,000 to $40,000, and this would not be the sort of thing that you would "bargain shop" for. This procedure was developed nearly 20 years ago, so it has been refined and studied to some degree. What has been found in these studies is:

1. Rapid opiate detox does not decrease time in detox.

There is no evidence that ultra-rapid opiate detoxification programs actually reduce the time you spend in withdrawal.

2. Rapid opiate detox does not decrease the intensity of withdrawal symptoms.

In some cases, rapid detox may reduce the intensity of symptoms during general anesthesia and the immediate recovery period. But in most cases, once awakened from anesthesia, people who choose ultra rapid detox report symptoms of discomfort comparable to those of more conventional detox procedures using a medically-assisted detox.

3. Rapid opiate detox is medically risky.

There have been several deaths associated with detox under anesthesia, particularly when performed outside a hospital. Rapid detox can provoke unconsciousness, transient confusion, or depressive mood. Even worse - pulmonary, psychiatric complications and metabolic complications from diabetes, all of which require hospitalization are possible. Of particular concern is vomiting during anesthesia (opiate withdrawal produces vomiting). Because of the significant increase in death risk, many specialists think the risks of rapid opiate detox outweigh the potential (and unproven) benefits.

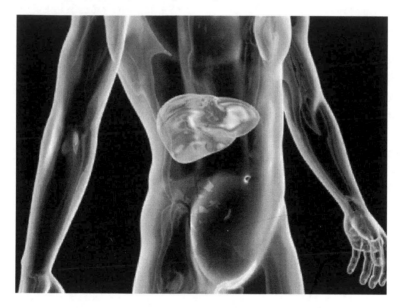

Although rapid opiate detox clinics report astonishing success and abstinence rates (as high as 100%), there has been little independent confirmation of these reports, and those few studies that have looked at relapse rates closely have found long-term abstinence rates very low. More realistic, and scientific, studies show something quite different. The Journal of Drug and Alcohol Dependence reported that "withdrawal symptoms were still present 24 hours after detoxification and 80 percent of the patients relapsed during a 6-month follow-up." This is similar to another study from Medizinische Klinik in Muchen, West Germany by Hirtl and Zilker, who found the procedure too dangerous to complete, that "No detoxification was finished within 48 hours," and concluded that "there is no obvious benefit from this method, whereas the risks are high."

Most addiction experts would agree that you can't just take out the drug and have a happy, well-adjusted person. You have to train them to get over the magical thinking and instant happiness, to earn their place in the sun - not to look for the lamp with a genie in it. This carries over to picking your method of detox from opiates as well. Quick fixes rarely work in the real world and getting clean has a lot to do with learning how to re-enter society and live in reality again.

The important thing to remember about ROD is that it is not a treatment for addiction. It is a treatment for withdrawal, and this is all. Because some studies have found that rapid detox followed by naltrexone did seem to keep patients from relapsing long enough to make those necessary lifestyle changes, it probably has its place in a comprehensive treatment approach. IF you decide to give Rapid Detox a try, do so with extreme caution. Be sure to have your overall health checked by an independent physician to ensure that you are truly a candidate. Also, do research on the particular facility that you are thinking of using and talk to former patients if you can. This is the best way to judge whether or not the actual procedure that you will be paying for and undergoing will be of benefit to you or not.

Ibogaine Treatment

When the light turns green, you go. When the light turns red, you stop. But what do you do when the light turns blue with orange and lavender spots? — Shel Silverstein, A Light in the Attic

Within a year after I first published this book, people began contacting me online, through my website and Facebook page, asking me about Ibogaine treatment. I've had some ask me if I've tried it (I haven't), whether or not I would recommend it, or even if I knew where they could purchase Ibogaine online to use at home (I don't). This has given me the opportunity to speak with quite a few people in the industry about Ibogaine and form some opinions about it. We spoke of addicts looking for "quick fixes" in the last chapter. This may be an example of another, albeit an interesting one.

Ibogaine is a psychedelic, a naturally occurring psychoactive substance that is found in plants of the Apocynaceae family, more specifically the root bark of Tabernanthe Iboga, which is native to central West Africa. As with many of the other substances discussed in this book, while many may not have heard of Ibogaine before, or until recently, it has been on the scene for quite some time.

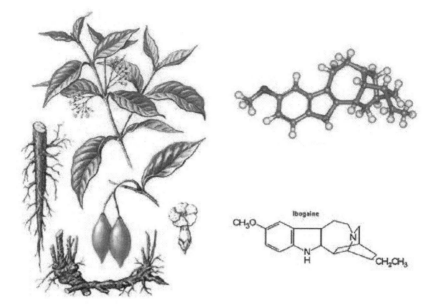

It is believed that Iboga has been used in spiritual practice and as rites of passage in Africa for thousands of years. However, it wasn't until the late 19th century that the activity was first observed by French and Belgian explorers. Synthesis of ibogaine first occurred in the 1960's, and it was in 1962 that the anti-addictive properties of the drug were inadvertently discovered by a 19-year old heroin addict, Howard Lotsof. Lotsof, who worked for S&L Laboratories, was part of an unofficial "study group" that evaluated experiences with various psychedelic drugs. What he found was that the ibogaine alleviated his craving for heroin and he was able to stop using without suffering the terrible consequences of withdrawal. In 1986, more than two decades later, he founded NDA International and started distributing ibogaine, under the name Endabuse, to addicts in Holland.

Since that time, ibogaine has been the subject of much study and even more controversy. Dr. Stanley Glick, a pharmacologist and neuroscientist, was one of the first researchers to test the drug on rats in the 1990's. Glick's results showed that ibogaine stopped cravings not only for morphine but also for alcohol, nicotine, cocaine and methamphetamine. What later studies also showed, however, were that ibogaine can cause irreparable brain damage, to the part of the brain the controls balance and motor skills. Other findings from the NIDA concluded that ibogaine increases the risk of seizures for people addicted to alcohol or benzodiazepines. The FDA had, at one time, granted funds for ibogaine research but those studies were immediately suspended in light of these studies.

So how exactly does ibogaine work? What is most interesting, and even more disturbing, is that those who have studied it still don't fully understand it. What ibogaine does is many fold. It alleviates the physical withdrawal symptoms of opiate detox by resetting and refreshing the opiate receptor sites. Ibogaine works to rebalance the brain chemistry and level out dopamine, serotonin, endorphins, and adrenaline to a pre-addicted state. There is also an anti-depressive effect that establishes a state of well-being, free from negative thought patterns.

Hallucinations are a big part of the ibogaine experience. As a psychedelic, the experience is described as having two phases: the visionary phase and the introspection phase. The visionary phase is like an awakened dream state and can last from 4 to 6 hours. Those who experience it report coming away with critical insight into the origins of their addiction or other unhealthy behavior patterns. Past events, even those not remembered consciously, may come forward to bring clarity and understanding. The introspective phase can last for the next 24-36 hours, wherein the information revealed is processed emotionally, and the body recuperates physically if necessary. Described by many as an incredibly intense experience, often with accompanied nausea, the Bwiti practitioners of Gabon call it "breaking open the head."

Long-term success with ibogaine is still unclear as there haven't been any controlled human trials of the drug used to treat addicts. It is clear that ibogaine blocks multiple receptors in the brain, yet this doesn't account for its long-term effects. The ability of the drug to lessen cravings is likely the result of its blocking the NMDA receptors, where drug craving activity has been linked. The long-term relief found from the drug could be explained by the fact that ibogaine is stored in fat tissue and slowly released into the bloodstream for up to six months.

What happens beyond that period of time is still being determined and studied.

As I stated earlier, this has become a controversial treatment for addiction in recent years. Some swear by it and others feel that it is either too dangerous or simply needs more study. Ibogaine has been illegal (Schedule I Substance) in the United States since 1967. It is also illegal in Australia, Norway, and Sweden. However, it remains unregulated in Canada, Mexico, Costa Rica, and many other countries. This has resulted in quite a few ibogaine treatment centers springing up in these countries where treatments are offered, costing anywhere from $2,000-$10,000 per multi-day session. There are also those who do illegal ibogaine treatments within the U.S. and people who take great risks and self-administer this drug at home. Despite the benefits to many, there ARE risks.

A very common effect, or side-effect, of taking a large dose of ibogaine is ataxia, which is a difficulty in coordinating muscle motion, making standing and walking challenging without assistance. Dry mouth, nausea, and vomiting are other side effects that may be experienced. There are quite a few conditions that are contra-indicated with regards to using ibogaine. These include any heart conditions, high blood pressure, pulmonary disorders, stomach problems, diabetes, or liver disease.

Since 1991, at least 19 people have died during or shortly after undergoing ibogaine treatment. Many of these patients did have heart problems, or they made the choice to combine ibogaine with their drug of choice. Three died at an ibogaine clinic in Tijuana. The fact of the matter is that ibogaine treatment because it is unregulated, can be very dangerous. However, because of the potential benefits of the drug, there may be a ray of hope in the very near future.

One of the long-time proponents of ibogaine, Dr. Stanley Glick, has been working on the legalization of ibogaine for over 20 years. Teaming up with chemist Martin Kuehne, the two have created a chemical called 18-MC (short for 18-methoxycoronaridine) that mimics ibogaine's effects on the brain, without the hallucinatory side effects. "Cocaine, meth, nicotine, morphine—we did the same studies with 18-

MC, and it worked as well or better than ibogaine," Glick says. Their company, Savant HWP, was given a $6.5 million 3-year grant by the NIDA in 2012 and began the first human trials of the drug in Brazil in October 2014.

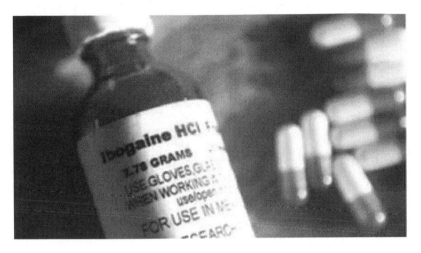

For those considering ibogaine as an addiction treatment right now, what's the verdict? Unfortunately, I can't answer that question for you. As a person who has been free from opiates for over a dozen years, it's easy enough for me to tell someone not to risk it. However, if I were in that deep, dark hole of addiction again (I do remember it) and unable to get clean by any other method, I can't say that I wouldn't try it either. I think that there are several important things to know about ibogaine. The first is that it is dangerous, and anyone who decides to take this risk should do their homework before taking the plunge. The second is that most reports that I have been reading about it indicate that it's really not a "cure." People do relapse, and quite frequently, after undergoing an ibogaine treatment. Brain chemistry is altered, perhaps for a time, but you are still left with the same person that was using copious amounts of opiates a day and then had to write a check for an uber-expensive detox. Unless there is follow up treatment and on-going support, I don't see this as any sort of magic bullet.

Of final note, being an addict (even one in recovery), I have a hard time visualizing the use of a drug as a "cure" for addiction. Remember, it was that insatiable appetite for drugs that got me here in the first place. I have read some very interesting things about ibogaine and people needing it for "maintenance." Now, most news stories and propaganda will sell you on the fact that it's a one-time treatment and then your cravings are gone for good. Dig a little deeper and there are, indeed, stories of ibogaine maintenance, using ibogaine "boosters" after so many weeks or months (who decides?), taking more ibogaine for "spiritual insight", and the need to do a full ibogaine "re-set" after a relapse or dark period. None of these sound like decisions that should be in the hands of an addict. I certainly couldn't do it.

Nobody stopped thinking about those psychedelic experiences. Once you've been to some of those places, you think, 'How can I get back there again but make it a little easier on myself?' - Jerry Garcia

Gabapentin for Opiate Withdrawal

We cannot, in a moment, get rid of habits of a lifetime. - Mahatma Gandhi

There is a lot of talk in addiction circles about using Gabapentin, also known as Neurontin, for opiate withdrawal. While there are some positive experiences with its use for this purpose, the drug has not been FDA approved as an effective treatment as research is in this area is still ongoing.

Gabapentin (brand name Neurontin) is a gamma-aminobutyric acid (GABA) analog that was originally developed for the treatment of epilepsy, pain relief, and neuropathic pain. Several studies have shown Neurontin to be effective for many patients who were suffering from the effects of opiate withdrawal. The drug can eliminate nerve pain as well as help with energy levels. Other patients may not see a significant change.

While Neurontin is considered to be a relatively safe drug and not subject to abuse, it does require a physician's prescription. Also, there is a possibility of withdrawal effects from the Neurontin itself when the medication is stopped, which may necessitate a tapering regimen. These factors should be weighed and discussed with a medical professional before deciding if Neurontin is a good fit for you.

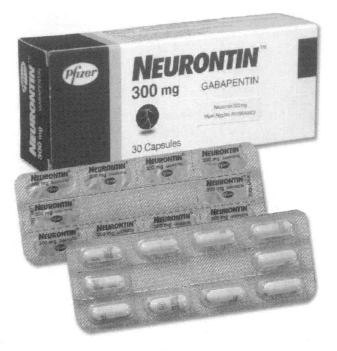

Seeking Medical Opiate Detox

Happiness is not something you postpone for the future; it is something you design for the present. -Jim Rohn

While generally not life threatening, detoxing from opiates is known as one of the toughest experiences because of the strong addictive pull that they have. When opiate use suddenly ceases during detoxification, the brain senses – often for the first time in years – a sharp, persistent chemical imbalance, resulting in strong cravings to re-engage in drug abuse. Additionally, psychological consequences, such as depression, anxiety and paranoia, also arise as the brain experiences a lack of mood-enhancing chemicals. This is why a medical detox is often used to help the patient get through withdrawal symptoms and get past the pull of opiate cravings.

There is also the issue of "polydrug use" to contend with in opiate addiction. Many opiate abusers, including myself, did not limit themselves to just opiates. Because of its sedating effects, many users also use stimulants such as amphetamines or cocaine to balance out the effects. I combined opiate use with benzos and sometimes alcohol in order regulate my sleep. Regardless, each drug poses unique health risks with prolonged use and has its own, sometimes conflicting, withdrawal symptoms. If you are, in fact, using multiple drugs to excess, you may wish to consider a medical detox for these reasons.

A medical detox is also often used if the patient has underlying pain issues that need to be managed. As is a particular concern with opiate painkiller addiction, many users have come to rely on the drugs for pain management, whether self-administered or not. However, once use stops, there is sometimes a "rebound effect", as pain becomes worse for a time due to lowered pain thresholds. A medical detox facility will be able to assist with pain management techniques as well as provide non-addictive alternatives during detox and treatment.

If there are other medical conditions or even co-occurring disorders, a medical detox may be in order. Any heart, respiratory or other major medical disorder should be managed in a medical setting as detox and withdrawal takes place. Likewise, many addicts have taken to self-medicate in order to treat their own psychiatric disorders. Customized care in these instances is important as detox from opiates takes place in order to manage these conditions properly.

Opiate withdrawal symptoms will vary and will depend on many factors including the particular drug abused, how much of it was consumed and for how long, and the patient's physical and psychological condition at the time of detox. The degree of medical intervention necessary will vary with the severity of withdrawal symptoms, including the intensity of cravings and mood disruption. Medical detox from opiates can also take place in either an outpatient or an inpatient basis, sometimes as the first phase of a residential addiction treatment program. Regardless, most medical detox programs have the following elements:

- **Assessment and Diagnostic Testing**
  Upon intake, patients will be asked to submit to a variety of psychological interviews or tests and physical exams in order to establish a baseline for treatment. Drug testing may be employed to allow addiction professionals to become apprised of any drug combinations present in the system, and to enable them to tailor the detox process to specific drugs of choice. Additionally, physical examinations may be performed. These tests serve to both prevent complications that could arise during detox and to ensure that patients receive medical attention for any physical damage they may have incurred during addiction. Psychological testing allows for identification of secondary mental health issues that may need concurrent treatment.

- **Medical Supervision**

  Many detoxification centers will provide medical supervision during the withdrawal process. Vital signs may be monitored to ensure ongoing health, physical checkups may be provided, and medications may be ordered to treat symptoms of withdrawal. Though rare, emergency medical assistance is sought if serious complications occur.

- **Medication Dispensation**

  Non-addictive medications are dispensed to treat any additional mental or physical health conditions uncovered during the detox or intake processes. Withdrawal symptoms are generally managed with sleep medications, natural remedies, non-addictive painkillers, antidepressants, anxiolytic drugs, and anti-nausea or anti-seizure medications. Clonidine is often prescribed to reduce anxiety, agitation, and muscle aches. In detox facilities that provide medical detox, specialized medicines aimed at prevention of relapse, reduction of withdrawal symptoms or alleviation of cravings may be dispensed. This is also where buprenorphine (i.e., - Suboxone) may be used in the detox process in order to taper the patient off of opiates.

In many cases, a medical detox from opiates is ideal. It is the safest method all around and provides the greatest chance of success. However, a few words of warning. Most people who OD on opiates do so when relapsing after detoxification. Once through the withdrawal process, your opiate tolerance (ability to handle large quantities of these drugs) diminishes greatly. Once fully detoxed, taking a dosage that would previously get you pleasantly high might now be enough to kill! Also, a medical detox is simply that - a detox. It is not a recovery program or any sort of treatment for the disease of addiction. This is merely the first step that gets you ready for more action, whether it be a treatment center or immediate immersion into an addiction support group.

While a medical detox seems like the ticket, it's not always possible for a variety of reasons. In some cases it is possible, and even necessary, to detox from opiates at home.

Opiate Detox at Home

*Find a place inside where there's joy, and the
joy will burn out the pain. -Joseph Campbell*

Who in their right mind would want to detox from opiates at home? A
LOT of people. So many, in fact, that I have written an entire book on
the matter (Safely Detox from Drugs and Alcohol at Home). Among
the reasons that people want to detox at home are:

Access - Detox facilities, particularly free and cheap ones, aren't as
easy to get into as they once were. In fact, many have waiting lists and
who wants to be on a waiting list to detox from drugs?

Privacy - Many people are still under the delusion that no one knows
about their little "problem" and don't want to have any record or trace
of a stay in a detox facility.

Time - Some folks seem to think that it will take less time to detox at
home or that they will be able to remain home and continue to meet
family obligations while going through this. If all that is required of
you is a pulse, this may be the case. Otherwise, you may wish to re-
think this one.

Is home detox from opiates possible? Yes, it is if you meet certain
conditions. One thing that you will need to consider before detoxing
from opiates is, why you were taking them in the first place. If you
were taking painkillers for a legitimate pain issue that still needs to be
managed, this would need to be addressed. There are some non-opiate
treatments for pain that exist, and you will need to consult with a
specialist, being brutally honest, in order to get the help that you need.

Home detoxification from drugs can be achieved under a lot of
circumstances, but not all. There is danger involved, and it is
exacerbated substantially by other physical and psychiatric disorders.
Complications from or by other factors may require that you be treated

in an inpatient facility for your safety. Some conditions that are of concern would be unstable diabetes, severe hypertension, and severe liver disease. These sorts of conditions would adversely affect the course of withdrawal and, conversely, withdrawal can aggravate these illnesses themselves. In addition, the presence of unstable psychiatric illness can complicate the management of withdrawal.

There may be difficulty in complying with medication regimens, and a psychiatric disorder can also intensify some symptoms of withdrawal such as confusion and agitation. A lot of times, alcohol and drugs are used to ease or relieve the symptoms of the psychiatric disorder. When the use stops, the original psychiatric symptoms that were suppressed and acute withdrawal can come forth simultaneously, and this needs to be managed in a controlled, professional setting.

Another consideration with opiates is the possibility of tapering. Some are able to do this successfully and then quit "cold turkey" from a much lower level opiates, lessening the withdrawal symptoms. If you do decide to try tapering with opiates, check out the hard rules for tapering listed at the end of this chapter and be sure to stick to them. Regardless, you will still need to prepare for the eventual withdrawal symptoms.

What to Expect When You Detox From Opiates at Home

Opiate withdrawal actually shares many symptoms with a bad case of the flu. Expect that you will lose your appetite, feel like sleeping or just be run down and suffer from general feelings of illness. Onset of symptoms will depend on the drug that you are detoxing from. The shorter the half-life of the drug, the quicker will be the onset of withdrawal. For example, heroin withdrawal will begin from 8-12 hours after the last dose, with symptoms lasting 5-7 days. The "acute phase" of detox from opiates can last up to 14 days, with the worst part being over in less than five days, depending on the drugs and amounts taken. Opiate withdrawal symptoms are characterized by:

- watery eyes
- runny nose
- anxiety

- insomnia
- dilated pupils
- gooseflesh
- muscle aches and joint pain
- abdominal cramps
- nausea and vomiting
- diarrhea
- hot and cold flashes

The post-acute withdrawal symptoms (PAWS) of insomnia, fatigue, and mild anxiety can last for many months after stopping taking the drugs. This is the period of time in which the body's opiate receptors heal, and the body learns to produce its own endorphins again. You can help this along through moderate exercise and good nutrition, as well as seeking out some sort of a support network (see final chapters of book on this).

Preparation for Detoxing From Opiates at Home

If you are planning to detox from any sort of opiates at home, consider this Detox Plan for detoxing from drugs at home:

- Take a look at yourself and why you are stopping (a little self-examination exercise)
- Make a List of all of the substances that you are using and quantities
- Call for a Doctor's Appointment if you are able
- Clear your Calendar (try for 2 weeks) - no work or other heavy obligations
- Get some support - Find family or friends that can help you through this
- Put your specific detox plan together based on your particular substance
- Get things to keep you occupied and entertained - books, movies, etc.
- Begin Detox process
- Keep a detox calendar and diary/journal to track your progress
- Don't use any more drugs or alcohol, or switch to something "new".
- Consider a support group afterwards (and even during if you can get out).

Aside from that, you'll need to make some special preparations with respect to detoxing from opiates at home.

Prepare the Environment

Again, one of the reasons that you are likely choosing to do this at home instead of in an institution is "comfort". If so, be sure that you have everything on hand to make your stay as comfortable, and safe, as possible. Detoxing from opiates and their withdrawal doesn't last as long as some others but don't expect to be hitting the mall or the beach while it's happening. You will be home for the duration so have something to keep yourself busy, whether it be books, movies, games, etc. Also, get rid of all of the drugs in the home. This should be a no-brainer, but it needs to be said. This is no joke. There is no "saving some for an emergency". If you've gone through the exercise in which you address "Why you are doing this", there shouldn't be much resistance here. Just get rid of it - toss it or give it away immediately. Trust me - you will not be able to resist the temptation once the withdrawal symptoms set in.

Support

You will need to line up a family member or friend to come and stay with you. This needs to happen from Day 1, as opiate detox can by psychologically very difficult. Probably after Day 3 or 4, you will be in the clear, and they can just check on you, but this will vary on a case by case basis.

Also, try to get an appointment with your family physician and request a prescription for a long-acting benzo such as Valium or Librium. Let your physician know what you are trying to do and that you simply want to take a reducing dose of this medication over the course of several days to lessen the withdrawal symptoms. Your doctor will help with proper dosage. However, if you already have Valium or Librium on hand (don't use other Benzos - they're not the same), this is merely an approximation (using Valium) or example for your reference only:

Day   1:   10mg   4   times   a   day
Day   2:   10   mg   4   times   a   day
Day   3:   5   mg   4   times   a   day
Day   4:   5   mg   4   times   a   day
Day   5:   5   mg   4   times   a   day
Day 6: 5 mg morning

If you are unable to get prescription medication to ease the symptoms, you can still find some comfort with over-the-counter medicines, supplements, vitamins and diet.

Here are some over-the-counter medications that you'll want to pick up and their uses:

- **Imodium (Loperamide)** - This is a must-have. It can help with the diarrhea that is likely to come and the gastrointestinal symptoms. Also, it is structurally similar to Demerol and can ease the overall harshness of the detox.
- **Benadryl (Diphenhydramine)** - This is another that is highly recommended. This can help with anxiety, restlessness, insomnia and the cold-like symptoms. Take 25-50 mg every 6 hours as needed.
- **Topical Creams containing Methyl Salicylate (Bengay, Icy Hot)** - for joint and muscle pain.
- **Calcium Carbonate (Tums)** - 1 to 2 tablets every 8 hours for abdominal pain and indigestion.
- **OTC Pain Reliever** such as Tylenol, Aleve, Aspirin or Ibuprofen.

As for vitamins and supplements, here are the things that you'll want to consider picking up if your budget allows (you had money for your drugs, didn't you?). Simply stick with the recommended dosages for all of these:

- Vitamin B6 caps
- Vitamin C
- Vitamin E
- Calcium
- Magnesium
- L-Glutamine
- Melatonin
- Valerian Root
- Passion Flower
- Milk Thistle

**If you can find the 1st five of these in a good multi-vitamin, that's fine too.

Diet

When we don't feel well or are anticipating not feeling well, it's tempting to grab a bunch of "comfort foods" and sustain ourselves on them. In this case, that would be a mistake. Chips and cookies are not going to give our liver the nutrients that it needs as it is over-working to detoxify our body from these mass amounts of opiates that have built up in it. You'll want to reduce the load on your liver by minimizing the processed foods and saturated fats that you put in your body. If you're not feeling well, it's ok to eat in small amounts but when you do eat something, eat the right things and stock up on some of this stuff:

- Fiber-rich fruits and vegetables
- Healthy proteins from chicken, fish, and eggs
- Plant proteins such as beans and peas
- Healthy fats from fish
- Nuts, seeds, extra virgin olive oil

Also, fluid intake is critical. Drink lots of water. Stay away from soda and coffee for at least three weeks. Your sleep patterns will already be disturbed, and these are not going to help. Green tea is also ok to drink and is good for its antioxidants and anti-inflammatory properties. It's ok to have a few sports drinks for flavor but stick mostly to good old fashioned water - and lots of it.

Other Activities

When the detox and withdrawal process starts, there is nothing else to do but ride it out and take it day by day or, if necessary, hour by hour. Don't forget to sleep when you are able, which for some people may be all the time, and to simply keep yourself occupied when you aren't. If you are prepared, you have some movies, books or something else to keep yourself busy for the next several days during the periods that you are unable to sleep. Use hot and cool baths to get comfortable as needed and as often as you like. If you have access to a swimming pool or hot tub and it helps, don't think twice about sitting in there all day long if you need to. Also, consider that a small amount of exercise can go a long way in making you feel better. Those cramped muscles can be stretched, and some endorphins can be released, which is so very important to your well-being. This can be as simple as a 5-10 minute walk. Finally, don't be too hard on yourself and don't forget why you are doing this. Hopefully, you went through some sort of exercise in self-examination before beginning this process so that you know why it is that you are giving up these drugs and what positive things you hope to gain from a life without them.

After Opiate Detox

The acute phase of opiate withdrawal can be over in as little as three days. That's just it, though, the withdrawal phase and the toxins leaving your body. It certainly wasn't fun, but all of that suffering would be for nothing if you were to walk right back out into the "real world" and resume use. This is an ongoing issue with opiate addiction and the list of things that opiate addicts simply do not understand include:

Addiction is a bona fide disease (Read the Disease Chapter Here - this is important)

Additional help or treatment is available and probably recommended (that Chapter is Here)

Finding a good support network is critical to remaining clean long term (Click Here to Read More About That)

Otherwise, you have successfully detoxed from opiates at home. Maybe this wasn't the first time. Regardless, it likely wasn't fun and not something that you would want to repeat or even do over and over again. If that's the case, please check out those final chapters in the book and the Resource Section before moving on.

Methadone and Suboxone Withdrawal Considerations

Believe that life is worth living and your belief
will help create the fact. -William James

While both methadone and buprenorphine (Suboxone) are used in detox and opiate maintenance programs they are, at the end of the day, opiates and many addicts find themselves enslaved to these drugs just as much, if not more so, than they were to their original drug of choice. While methadone has been around for many years as a legal maintenance drug for opiate addicts, buprenorphine is a newer drug on the market used for both detox and maintenance. Both drugs have their uses, and both are widely abused. Even many addicts who don't abuse the drugs and take them for maintenance purposes reach a point where they simply want to get off of them and don't know how.

The unique difficulty here lies in the extreme hold that these drugs have on their users. This is largely to do with their action and their half-lifes. Both methadone and Suboxone occupy your opiate receptors quite vigorously. They also have very long half-lifes, which is the time that it takes the drug to metabolize in your system, or reduce its concentration in your bloodstream by 50%. A drug with a longer half-life will, by definition, have a longer detox period.

All opiates, long-acting or not, serve to mimic the natural painkilling neurotransmitters in the brain. However, in long-term use of methadone and suboxone, the brain produces less of these substances, causing detox from them to be quite painful and prolonged. While highly unpleasant, methadone withdrawal and suboxone detox are not considered to be life-threatening. This does not mean that you wouldn't benefit from a controlled, medically supervised environment. On the contrary, a formal detox facility would make your experience much more comfortable.

One thing that you will need to consider before detoxing from methadone or suboxone is, why you were taking it in the first place. If you were taking the drug for a legitimate pain issue that still needs to be managed, this will need to be addressed. Methadone is now more commonly used for pain management than it was in the past, which has opened it up to greater diversion and abuse. There are some non-opiate treatments for pain that exist, and you will need to consult with a specialist, being brutally honest, in order to get the help that you need.

Another consideration with methadone and suboxone is the recommendation of tapering, whether you are doing this on your own or with medical supervision. Some are able to do this successfully and then quit "cold turkey" from a much lower level of the drug, lessening the withdrawal symptoms. If you do decide to try tapering with methadone or suboxone, check out the hard rules for tapering at the end of this chapter and be sure to stick to them. It is highly recommended that you taper your dose over as long a period as you are able before you stop taking it completely. A general guide for methadone is to lower your dose anywhere from 2mg-5mg per month until you are down to zero. You can do this faster if you must, but remember that everyone's body is different and what may be an easy detox and taper for one person could be very difficult for someone else. Regardless, you will still need to prepare for the eventual withdrawal symptoms.

Methadone and suboxone withdrawal actually shares many symptoms with a bad case of the flu. Expect that you will lose your appetite, feel like sleeping or just be run down and suffer from general feelings of illness. The onset of symptoms may not appear for 48 hours or more because of the long half-life of the drug and the amount that has built up in your system. The "acute phase" of detox can last up to 14 days, with the worst part being over in less than seven days, depending on the dosage and frequency taken. Methadone and suboxone withdrawal symptoms are characterized by:

- watery eyes
- runny nose

- anxiety
- insomnia
- dilated pupils
- gooseflesh
- muscle aches and joint pain
- abdominal cramps
- nausea and vomiting
- diarrhea
- hot and cold flashes

The post-acute withdrawal symptoms (PAWS) of insomnia, fatigue, and mild anxiety can last for many months after stopping taking the drugs. This is the period of time in which the body's opiate receptors heal, and the body learns to produce its own endorphins again. You can help this along through moderate exercise and good nutrition, as well as seeking out some sort of a support network (see final chapters of book on this).

I have, myself, detoxed off of methadone "cold turkey" with no tapering. This certainly wasn't ideal and was far from pleasant. I actually knew nothing about the dangers or potential severity of detoxing off of a long-acting opiate on my own at the time. What I did know was that a bed had come available for me in a treatment center that did not allow me to be on methadone or anything of the sort when I went in. I desperately wanted to get clean, so I bit the bullet and went for it. The withdrawal symptoms didn't start until several days later and lasted for about ten days. I don't remember what my dose of methadone was when I walked away from the clinic for the last time (I was using it as prescribed for opiate maintenance), but I do remember not being able to keep down even a sip of water for close to a week, the abdominal pain and the insomnia. These are things that I am not likely to forget for a very long time.

If you plan to do this at home, follow the general guidelines that were established in the prior chapter for opiate detox at home. Otherwise, be sure consult with a physician and it would be best to have someone else put your detox plan and tapering schedule together for you. At some point, you will reach what is called a "jumping off dose," where you will stop taking the drug altogether. Regardless of that level, expect that there will be some form of withdrawal symptoms, and likely PAWS, that will ensue after you "jump." While this doesn't happen for everyone, it is pretty common.

To Taper or Not - and Hard Rules for Tapering

If you've done some research online, you may have run across some groups that recommend "tapering" off your drug of choice before stopping completely. There are different schools of thought to this and, frankly, logic doesn't always come into play when it comes to talking about addiction and addictive behavior. Yes, it all sounds well and good in theory but how does it work in practice? Not always very well.

Say you are taking 30 painkillers a day (opiates) and someone recommends that you start tapering off and go to 25 or 20 a day. That may be easier said than done, especially if you have those other 5 or 10 in your possession. Regardless of your desire to "quit" or not, this is not an easy proposition, and some are more successful with this than others. If you feel that you can trust someone else with your substances (many can't) and can have them rationed out to you, this may work. Otherwise, the craving may still get the best of you, and you go straight to a source for more anyway. If you do decide to try tapering, here are some **"Hard Rules for Tapering"** that you will need to stick to:

1. Line up a tough trusted friend, spouse or significant other who will be in charge of your meds and will dole them out to you. This person will have to hold the line no matter how much you whine and try to manipulate.
2. Follow a set schedule. The schedule should be written out and turned over to the person administering the meds.
3. Approach the tapering from a clinical point of view (yes, I know this is difficult).
4. The heavier doses should be first thing in the morning and last of the evening
5. Do not attempt to delay a dosing time and hold off. This will cause a rebound effect that you don't want - i.e., - you will crave more.

6. Before starting your schedule, count up the exact number of pills you'll require from start to finish...and FLUSH all extraneous pills

7. Before starting your schedule, go to every hiding spot you have and discard those pills. Check jacket pockets, glove compartments, underwear drawers, shoes, handbags, etc. You get the idea. A nasty surprise after you've finished your taper is not something you want to encounter.

8. Hold nothing back "just in case." That's a reservation, and it will do you in.

9. Do not rush the taper. Don't get brave. Brave is often foolish and looking for that instant gratification of instant "clean." It won't work.

10. No yo-yo-ing (spiking). An extra pill will interrupt your process and reset your progress. This is highly counter-productive. The goal is to titrate steadily downward.

11. No chewing or snorting. Take them the old fashioned way...with a glass of water and swallow.

12. Cut off all connections; that dealer, that doctor, that pharmacy...whomever. They no longer exist for you. Shut the door firmly. Delete all numbers from your phone.

13. Have no expectation that this will be a comfortable process. Accept it for what it is...a rite of passage to freedom.

One instance where tapering is recommended a lot is in the case of Benzos because the detox and withdrawal from them is quite severe, dangerous and prolonged. If you are looking to detox from Benzos on your own (not recommended), or even from a laundry list of drugs, I highly recommend picking up my other book for some more detailed instructions. Tapering is also used when one is attempting to get free of Methadone or Suboxone, which are other dangerous drugs to stop "cold turkey". Clinics will taper patients for a long time before releasing them. Otherwise, methadone and Suboxone withdrawal is also severe and very prolonged.

If you are in one of these situations where tapering may be of benefit to you, consult your physician before starting. Even where other drugs are used in the detox process, they are tapered so as not to cause an additional dependence situation. The only times that I was even remotely successful with tapering were when I had a limited supply of a drug and more or less was "rationing" myself off of the last of it over a period of time. Otherwise, keep in mind that addiction is a very powerful disease and tapering, by itself, is oftentimes easier said than done. Honestly, unless you think you have a very good reason for attempting this, just jump into detox and be done with it.

Tips for Managing Cravings

Believe you can and you're halfway there. -
Theodore Roosevelt

Cravings are urges to drink or use drugs. These urges are a normal part of any addiction and are commonplace during withdrawal. They can also pop up months or even years after you stop using drugs. Here are some important things to remember about cravings and some ways to deal with them.

What You Should Know About Cravings:

- They are not caused by a lack of willpower or motivation. It doesn't mean that you are doing something wrong or failing to do something right.
- Cravings don't mean that your detox and withdrawal aren't working.
- Cravings pass. These urges are not constant and are only severe for a very short period of time before they settle down to a more controllable level.
- Cravings can be triggered by physical or psychological discomfort. Managing these can help manage the onset and severity of cravings.

Things You Can Do to Manage Cravings:

- Remind yourself that cravings are "temporary". In fact, if the urge to use is very strong, simply put the decision off for an hour, and the feelings will likely subside.

- Identify cues or "triggers" that may have brought on the cravings. They could people, places or things that remind you of using. Re-direct your mental energy towards ways in which you can avoid these same triggers in the future.
- Remind yourself of why you stopped taking the drug in the first place. This would be the time to re-list the negative effects that the drug use had on your life and also list the positive things that you stand to gain by staying clean.
- Call on others for help. This is where a Support Network comes in, supportive family members and friends that support your recovery.
- Use your spirituality to get through cravings. Prayer and meditation can help calm the mind and bring the focus back into what you have achieved so far and what lies ahead in your recovery.

Now that we've covered some basic things to know about detoxing from opiates let's explore what needs to be done afterwards in order to remain clean and begin a life of recovery from addiction.

Going to Treatment or Not for Opiate Addiction...

If you want what you've never had, you must do what you've never done.

While the first step in recovery from opiate addiction is making the decision to stop, there is still a lot of ground to cover and action to be taken before the addict starts to feel some relief. Actually stopping using is HUGE and is no small feat. This is either accomplished through a home detox or some formal detox program that may or may not be integrated into a formal treatment program. The fact of the matter is that simply getting the drugs out of our system isn't enough to recover from addiction. Many of us, myself included, have suffered from the delusion that we were simply trapped in a "physical addiction" and, once free, would be able to resume living life just as we had before all of this nonsense started. Wrong! There is an "invisible line" that has been crossed, and you will never be able to go back to that "old life". That's the bad news. The good news is that you absolutely can recover from this and lead an even better life than you had ever imagined. Yes, it sounds ridiculous and like a bunch of "hocus pocus" right now, but stick with me here. There is light at the end of the tunnel after a bit more education and self-discovery.

Most addicts assume that they have to go to treatment to recover and get better. I certainly did and passed through an endless stream of rehabs in my journey. In fact, if you spend any time in front of the television (most do), then we are taught that in order to "get clean and sober", you have to go to rehab. This isn't necessarily the case, yet the treatment center industry has seen a recent "boom" in the past few decades as getting clean and sober is now all the rage. So, are these fancy places necessary to start your road to recovery? This is hotly debated, and the answer is different for each individual. Many people are able to get clean and sober and stay that way with the help of 12 Step programs alone - no rehab. However, in our fast-paced society, with all of life's demands, treatment centers certainly have carved out their niche in the "getting clean" process and have some very real value.

It may be that you haven't been given a choice. The edict to "go to rehab" could have been handed down by an employer, a family member or even a judge. If that's the case, the question has been answered for you. Otherwise, if you are still pondering whether or not to go to treatment, there are several different types of treatment centers to choose from, and they certainly do have their benefits if you decide to go.

Different Types of Treatment Centers

Sometimes the wrong choices bring us to the right places.

Choices abound as to what sort of treatment center, if any, is going to be right for you. You will need to decide between Inpatient or Outpatient, Private or Public and, in some cases, Co-Ed or Single Sex treatment centers.

Inpatient vs. Outpatient - Many people are inclined to select "outpatient" right off the bat because we are also inclined to downplay the seriousness of our situation and the means necessary to recover from it. Some people are able to successfully participate in treatment programs on a part-time basis while continuing to live at home, manage their family lives and keep their jobs. These people are exceptions to the rule, however. There are other outpatient treatment programs that simply have you go to treatment during the day and return to your home (and family) at night. Again, depending on your circumstances, this may be a viable option. For many, and for a lot of reasons, it's not for a lot of people.

Inpatient drug and alcohol treatment is more the norm for quite a few reasons. This option dictates that the individual moves into some sort of dorm-like setting and receives 24/7 care and supervision. Some treatment centers allow for private and semi-private rooms while others dictate that you will essentially take what you are given. Inpatient treatment is the ideal choice for someone who needs a place to focus entirely on their addiction and developing their recovery program.

Private vs. Public - Regardless of the previous differences, you will run into rehab centers that are both Private and Publicly funded. Different treatment funding sources include:

- Private: Non-profit, or For Profit

- State or Locally Funded

- Low-Cost Treatment Centers

- Free Rehabs (Charity Rehabs)

While the Free, Low Cost and Government Funded treatment centers sound great (they are, I got sober in one), it's important to note that many also have long waiting lists. Another difference, although not true in all cases, may be the size of groups in therapy sessions, with smaller groups in Private facilities and larger groups in publicly funded rehabs. Also, do not expect to get into any sort of private or semi-private room in a public facility. In retrospect, being "pampered" did nothing to get me clean. I did find the many waiting lists very disheartening though when I was finally "ready" for this and just couldn't get in anyplace. So, if you are looking at Private treatment centers and possible ways to finance it, consider these:

- **Health Insurance** - most "good" health insurance policies provide for some form of substance abuse treatment. If you have a really good policy, you may be able to get an inpatient treatment program paid for

- **Family Members** - you may already have family members offering to pay to get you sober. I did. I even had friends of family willing to chip in at one point.

- **Sell stock or take money from your 401k** - If you're unemployed, in jail or dead, there will be no "retirement" to save for, right?

- **Home Equity Loan** - If you are lucky enough to still be holding onto your home, consider this.

- **Sell stuff, even your car** - Chances are you have expensive toys you haven't been using because of you've been putting all of your efforts into drinking and drugging. Sell them. You don't need a car if you're not sober. It's a hazard.

- **Substance Abuse Treatment Loan** - Yes, they have these now.

Co-ed vs Same Sex Treatment Centers - I've been to both and it didn't make a difference to me either way. However, if you have been the victim of abuse and think that you would feel safer in a same-sex facility, by all means, check them out.

Drug-Specific Treatment Centers - Do an internet search for a treatment center that specializes in opiate addiction and you are sure to find plenty. Rest assured, these are marketing ploys. Nothing else. I know that we all like to think that our particular problem, and thus our needs, are unique and many rehabs will feed into that belief to get you in the door. The fact of the matter is that there is no difference in your treatment requirements, other than detox, than someone who's drug of choice is alcohol, cocaine, meth, marijuana or spray paint.

Different sorts of rehab centers may work better for different people, or any of them may work for the same person should that person simply be ready. It's all a matter of perspective. Sara, a student from Oregon who's been clean for five years, says that not all rehabs are created equal. "Inpatient was necessary," she says, "I don't know what my life would look like otherwise. But outpatient was ridiculous - it's not real. Maybe it helps people who just need a place to 'be good' for a while, but it isn't enough for strong users. If you've got a real problem, you have to go away for at least a month, because it's hard to take it in if you're still living in the same environment. Outpatient was just something to keep me busy for a few hours." In still another case, Abby, a 35 year-old advertising copywriter, credits outpatient with saving her life. "I wasn't willing to take a leave of absence from work to go away somewhere and I wasn't willing to go to AA," she recalls. "I signed up for outpatient, went there every day after work, and slowly acclimated to the idea of AA there. It gave me a version of the program - sort of AA lite - because we had groups where we talked about sobriety, but it was a small, safe environment. I don't think I'd be sober today had I not gone."

I have been to outpatient treatment centers, inpatient treatment centers, co-ed, same sex, private and public. They all had value and any one of them could have gotten me clean had I been ready to be there and cooperate. Every time, until the last one, I had been forced to go and at no time did anyone present to me the pro's and con's of going to treatment so that I could make some sort of informed decision on the matter.

The Pros and Cons of Going to Rehab

You are free to make whatever choice you want, but you are not free from the consequences of the choice.

When I first started hitting the treatment centers, I didn't see any "Pro's" to this nonsense whatsoever. I did not want to be there, did not think that I had a problem like the rest of the folks in that place did and felt very inconvenienced by the whole thing. Quite a few treatment centers and many years of sobriety later, it's much easier to see their benefit. However, I do clearly see what the Con's are in committing to these institutions. Here are a few:

Con's of Going to Treatment

Time - Yes, you are committing a substantial amount of your time to this program. You are committing literally ALL of your time if you elect to go to an inpatient treatment center. This means that family and work responsibilities need to be re-arranged. In many cases, some or all of those have "dissolved" on their own because of our drinking and drugging activities.

Cost - Most people would agree that this is the biggest downside to treatment, particularly private rehabs. Inpatient programs can cost upwards of $1,000 per day and outpatient programs are not cheap either. Publicly funded programs are more affordable, but there are often many hoops to jump through to qualify and get into these programs.

Pro's of Going to Treatment

Structured Environment - One of the biggest benefits of attending treatment, primarily residential (or inpatient), is that you are provided with a safe, structured environment that is free of distractions and temptations. This will give you a window of opportunity to get clean and sober (post-detox) and learn how to live life without drugs and alcohol. This structured environment is designed to be essentially free of the daily stressors of work, home and family so that you can focus only on your recovery.

Establish Network of Positive People - Attending treatment, inpatient or outpatient, gives you the opportunity to form new friendships and bonds with other like-minded, positive people. These are relationships that can be the beginning of your sober support network.

Learning Better Holistic Health - If giving up drinking and drugs were enough, this would be a much shorter book. However, the real purpose of recovery is to learn how to live a happy and healthy life without drugs and alcohol. Learning to treat yourself well in all respects is something that you can learn in treatment, such as eating right, being physically active and taking care of your mental and spiritual well-being.

Save Money - Wait, what?! Didn't we just say in the "Con's" that "cost" was a downside to going to treatment? Well, yes we did. BUT, let's look at the big picture here. The amount of money that you will save in long run by getting, and staying clean and sober, is astounding compared to continuing with that financial minefield of active addiction. Many people are blown away when they see the financial figures tied to their disease. I'm not just talking about the money spent on drugs and alcohol (count this, though). Add in jobs lost, promotions lost, missed opportunities, legal fees, smashed cars, foreclosed homes, and so on. Looking at it this way, the cost of a stint at that fancy rehab may not look as outrageous as it did earlier.

Save Your Life - For some, it really does boil down to this. It's simply a matter of life or death. Without some real, structured help, the end is imminent.   A lot of addicts and alcoholics run to treatment in hopes that they will "save" something or get their lives back. What many find is that they have been given an entirely new life that is infinitely better than anything they could have ever dreamed possible.

Making the Most of Rehab If You Decide to Go

...we do not always like what is good for us in this world. -Eleanor Roosevelt

If you make the decision to go to a treatment facility, good for you! You are giving yourself a gift that will not only come back to you tenfold but to those you know and love as well, even if your relationships aren't as you would want them to be right now. As we reviewed earlier, there are so many different types of treatment facilities, so it's not possible to give you a perfect run down of what to expect. However, here arc a few words of wisdom so that you can make the most of your stay:

There will be no locks on the doors. This doesn't work, not even for a second, if you're not willing, so you can walk away at any time. Even if you are court ordered to be at a place, they'll just come and pick you up to face your consequences at a later date should you bolt. Check your willingness level at the door, and thereafter frequently, and commit to stay for whatever term is recommended.

If you go - From my experience with the revolving doors of many treatment centers, these are my words of wisdom. First and foremost, check the attitude at the door. This is one thing that I took in with me and held onto through nearly all of my stays, except for the last one. It did me no favors. Thinking that I still knew what was best for me, after the shit storm that I had just made of my life was ludicrous. Also, demanding that I be given respect and attention when I felt I needed it was just as insane. I had to come to a place where I finally understood that I knew absolutely nothing about how to recover from this disease and that these people were clearly authorities on the subject. So probably, I should just let them do their job and listen to someone else for a change. Once I did this - made this mental shift (some would call it "surrender"), going to treatment was a blessing for me and I made the most of every single opportunity that was put in front of me to learn and to start my recovery. Yes, this included going to NA or AA, which I also resisted for a long time.

The Importance of a Support Group in Addiction Recovery

Separate reeds are easily broken; but bound together they are strong and hard to break apart. -The Midrash

Yes, we are talking about a 12 Step Group here, NA or AA preferably. There are alternative "recovery groups" out there, but this author knows absolutely nothing about them or their success rates. What I do know is that 12 Step Groups work 100% for people that follow the directions 100%. That's the key. Many people, myself included, have avoided getting clean and sober simply because they feared "joining" NA or AA. I had no concept of what these groups were or just how something like this could possibly be of any assistance to me. In fact, the notion that I would have to "join" and participate in anything was appalling. I didn't understand what AA was, and there is always the fear of the unknown.

So, what is AA then? What it is, really, is a multi-faceted program that incorporates meetings, fellowship and working a 12-step program in order to bring about a change in the addict or alcoholic and provide continued growth and support. (NA is the same - they just change some words around in the "steps" and the literature is different.) AA was founded in 1935 by Bill Wilson (known as Bill W) and Dr. Robert Smith (known as Dr. Bob), based on the main principle of one alcoholic sharing their experiences with another. Within four years, their basic text called "Alcoholics Anonymous" (aka The Big Book) was published, and membership blossomed. Today, there are over 2 million members of AA worldwide (over 1/2 of these in the U.S.) and over 115,000 registered AA Groups. In fact, there are now over 200 different fellowships that employ the "12 Steps" for recovery from AA (altered to fit). Hard to argue with those numbers.

The choice of whether to join AA or NA is also hugely confusing to many whose "drug of choice" was mainly opiates, as was mine. This had me scratching my head for quite some time and I spent about the first year going to both meetings and asking a lot of questions before deciding to attend AA exclusively. Here's why, and please note that this is only my story, but I am certainly not alone. I was able to see, quite easily, that I was undoubtedly also an alcoholic as I began drinking at 15 and drank to excess until I found opiates in my early 20s. Had I not switched to drugs, I would have continued drinking and unfortunately it would probably have taken me longer to hit my bottom. I also found a stronger recovery message in AA. While the members in NA meetings tended to speak about "using drugs", the members in AA meetings tended to share more about "living sober" and this is what I needed to hear (and still do) on a daily basis. I have found, over the years, that AA has given me everything I need to live a clean, sober, and very fulfilling life. I have also found that there are many, many people like myself in AA who were addicted to drugs in their past, yet have found a warm and welcoming home in AA. Regardless, there are many who also have lasting recovery in NA and I urge everyone to find their own path.

Giving up control is difficult and joining a "Support Group" of any sort is giving up another layer of control with respect to this disease. Believe me - I get it. I had to get to a place in my life and with my disease where I finally understood that my way wasn't working in any way, shape or form and I became willing to try something else. Recovery from addiction happens on many levels: physical, mental, emotional and spiritual. The programs of AA and NA address these different levels of recovery through their different facets of: attending meetings, getting a sponsor, working the 12 steps, spiritual principles, and involvement in the fellowship. In doing these things, old habits are broken, new (healthy) habits are formed, and we are able to take a deeper look at the causes and conditions underlying our long using careers. All of this is done in some manner that taps into the mechanisms that counter the complex neurological and psychological processes through which this disease wreaks its havoc. Better yet, it's done through the power of "the group". Psychologists have long known that one of the best ways to change human behavior is to gather people with similar problems into groups instead of treating them individually. This is one of AA's precepts.

Whether it is the initial act of "surrender", the group support setting, the self-awareness that comes from working the Steps, or the close relationships in the fellowship through helping others that are the key components to the addict's recovery (one or all of these), no one knows. What we do know, however, is that despite all we've learned over the past few decades about psychology, neurology, and human behavior, contemporary medicine has yet to devise anything that works markedly better. "In my 20 years of treating addicts, I've never seen anything else that comes close to the 12 steps," says Drew Pinsky, the addiction-medicine specialist who hosts VH1's Celebrity Rehab. While AA may not be a miracle cure for all, people who become deeply involved in the program stay clean and sober and do well over the long haul, and this starts with attending meetings. Check out the Resources Section at the end of the book for links to various 12 Step Groups. It starts by attendance at the first meeting and goes from there. Addiction is not something that can, or should, be battled alone.

There are no problems we cannot solve together, and very few that we can solve by ourselves. -Lyndon B. Johnson

Afterward

Opiate Addiction was released just over three years ago and has sold thousands of copies in a very short time. In fact, it is now on the shelves in bookstores and being bought in bulk by various institutions. That's pretty telling, and this isn't a masterpiece by any means. It's a fairly quick read, by design, and meant to give straightforward information about the nature of opiate addiction, its seriousness, and a formula for recovery. I hope I've accomplished that and helped even just one person to find the way out of this mess because it seems so hopeless when you are in it.

Just in the past year, as addiction has continued to spin out of control in this country we've seen progress on several fronts. Communities are beginning to see the merits of decriminalising addiction and providing help to addicts as opposed to punishing and shaming them. Pill mill doctors, on the other hand, are being taken off of the street and given their just dues. After President Obama announced some sweeping drug policy changes at the end of 2015, he followed that up in 2016 by asking for $1.1 billion in funding to fight opioid and heroin abuse over the next two years. The FDA has even unveiled some sweeping drug policy changes in 2016, which could alter the way that this country approaches prescription painkillers going forward.

For those still stuck in the quicksand of opiate addiction, know that there is hope. Being clean and sober over 14 years now, I can tell you several things. One is that the game has changed, and it's mind-boggling how prolific opiate addiction has become. I feel as if I were almost a trailblazer in the 90's with that stuff (and not in a good way)! The second is that life is so much better and so much more rewarding without the drugs and all that came with them. It may not seem possible while buried in addiction and all of the behaviors and fears that go along with it, but it's true. All it takes is the willingness to try something different, and your world can turn into something beyond your wildest dreams. This is my hope and prayer for anyone and everyone suffering from opiate addiction. If you don't have any hope right now, you can have some of mine.

Useful Resources

Treatment Centers

There are no "public" websites that offer treatment center, detox and sober living directories. Unfortunately, any site you find will be filled with "sponsored results". This means rehabs that have paid for ad space. That's not always a bad thing, just not an unbiased thing. The best site I've found is Sober.com. You'll get the sponsored results in your search but you will also get all of the public listings as well, including the government-funded (some free) facilities.

Another Treatment Center Resource (http://www.drugrehabcenters.org/ByState/Drug_Rehab_Centers_With_Sliding_Scale_Fees.htm) - This one also lists the treatment centers that either have a sliding fee scale, accept public funds or are free.

Links to Opioid Treatment Centers by State (http://dpt2.samhsa.gov/treatment/directory.aspx), including Methadone and Buprenorphine treatment.

Support Groups

Narcotics Anonymous (http://www.na.org/)

Alcoholics Anonymous (http://aa.org/)

Heroin Anonymous (http://www.heroinanonymous.org)

Nar-Anon Family Groups (http://www.nar-anon.org/naranon/)
Al-Anon Websites (http://www.al-anon.alateen.org/)
Cocaine Anonymous (http://ca.org/)
Adult Children of Alcoholics (http://www.adultchildren.org/)
Co-Dependence Anonymous (CoDA) (http://www.coda.org/)

Mental Health

National Institute of Mental Health (http://www.nimh.nih.gov/)

Results of biomedical research on mind and behavior.

National Alliance for the Mentally Ill (http://www.nami.org/)

Support for consumers with mental illness

Substance Abuse & Mental Health Services Administration (http://www.samhsa.gov/)

United States Department of Health & Human Services

Government Resources

Single-State Agency (SSA) Directory: (http://www.recoverymonth.gov/Recovery-Month-Kit/Resources/Single-State-Agency-SSA-Directory.aspx) Prevention and Treatment of Substance Use and Mental Disorders – A list of State offices that can provide local information and guidance about substance use and mental disorders, treatment, and recovery in your community.

AMVETS (http://www.amvets.org/) This organization provides support for veterans and the active military in procuring their earned entitlements. It also offers community services that enhance the quality of life for this Nation's citizens.

Professionals

Intervention Project for Nurses (http://www.ipnfl.org/)

Help for professionals with chemical dependencies.

International Lawyers in Alcoholics Anonymous (ILAA) (http://www.ilaa.org/)

This organization serves as a clearinghouse for support groups for lawyers who are recovering from alcohol or other chemical dependencies.

International Pharmacists Anonymous (IPA) (http://home.comcast.net/~mitchfields/ipa/ipapage.htm)

This is a 12-step fellowship of pharmacists and pharmacy students recovering from any addiction.

Other

This Center for Substance Abuse Prevention widget (http://www.samhsa.gov/about/csap.aspx) includes a variety of updates on activities relating to underage drinking which is updated regularly with local, state, and national articles published by online sources.

NCADD: (http://ncadd.org/) The National Council on Alcoholism and Drug Dependence, Inc. (NCADD) and its Affiliate Network is a voluntary health organization dedicated to fighting the Nation's #1 health problem – alcoholism, drug addiction and the devastating consequences of alcohol and other drugs on individuals, families and communities.

American Council for Drug Education (http://www.acde.org/)

Educational programs and services for teens, parents, and educators

The Heroin Awareness Campaign (Curiosity + Heroin: Not Even Once) (http://www.not-even-once.com/)

The Heroin Awareness Campaign was implemented because of the great need to get the word out that heroin has become a problem of epidemic proportion. The campaign's message that curiosity + heroin is a deadly combination features the not-even-once.com website as a means to heighten awareness and bring relevant and important information to those visiting the website.

AlcoholScreening.org - Website offering an online screening tool to assess drinking patterns. The website offers visitors free confidential online screenings to assess their drinking patterns, giving them personalized feedback and showing them if their alcohol consumption is likely to be within safe limits. AlcoholScreening.org was developed by Join Together, a project of the Boston University School of Public Health, and was launched in April 2001. The website also provides answers to frequently asked questions about alcohol and health consequences, and provides links to support resources and a database of local treatment programs. Disclaimer: This site does not provide a diagnosis of alcohol abuse, alcohol dependence or any other medical condition. The information provided here cannot substitute for a full evaluation by a health professional, and should only be used as a guide to understanding your alcohol use and the potential health issues involved with it.

About the Author

Taite Adams grew up everywhere. The only child of an Air Force navigator and school teacher, moving around became second nature by grade school. By age 20, she was an alcoholic, drug addict and self-proclaimed egomaniac. Pain is a great motivator, as is jail, and she eventually got sober has found peace and joy in this life beyond measure.

At the age of 42, Taite published her first book titled "Kickstart Your Recovery". Now permanently Free on Amazon, the book answers many of the questions that she herself had but was afraid to ask before giving up the fight with addiction and entering recovery over a decade prior. Since, she has published four other recovery books, including her bestselling book on Opiate Addiction, and has moved into the broader spirituality and self-help genres.

Leading a spiritual life is all about choices. The practice of spiritual principles and the willingness to remain teachable are the key ingredients for growth. As a spiritual seeker and reader of the self-help genre herself, Taite appreciates and respects each and every person who takes the time to read her works and respond with reviews and comments. For more information on books, upcoming releases, and to connect with the author, go to http://www.taiteadams.com.

Check out our active Facebook Page: <u>Taite Adams Recovery Books</u>.

As you begin your Road to Recovery, please check out Taite's first book, <u>Kickstart Your Recovery</u>, available in both Kindle (where's it is Permanently FREE) and Paperback.

Should you require additional assistance with your home detox, be sure to pick up Taite's popular book, <u>Safely Detox From Alcohol and Drugs at Home</u>, also on Amazon.com.

Benzodiazepine Addiction is fast becoming a problem of epidemic proportions world-wide, and it's one that crosses all age barriers. Beyond Benzos examines this serious prescription drug addiction and its complicated detox options.

Senior Addiction refers to the growing issue of alcoholism and drug addiction amongst older adults. As baby boomers hit retirement age in record numbers, the instances of overdose deaths and new treatment admissions in this age group is skyrocketing. Read about the particular issues with regards to addiction and treatment in this particular class.

If you or a loved one are in recovery from alcoholism or addiction and want to learn more about emotional sobriety, check out Taite's book titled Restart Your Recovery, also on Amazon.com.

Another popular emotional sobriety subject is that of boundaries, which can be a challenge for anyone but particularly those in recovery who may not have had healthy relationships in the past. These issues and more are addressed in Taite's latest book, Boundaries in Recovery: Emotional Sobriety Through Setting Personal Limitations.

It's hard to miss mention in the media of the drug Molly and the controversy surrounding its use and it's ingredients. There is plenty of confusion there as well. Check out Taite's book, called Who is Molly? for the latest info on this drug and it's dangers.

Have you ever wanted to learn more about Ego? Taite's latest personal development book, titled E-Go: Ego Distancing Through Mindfulness, Emotional Intelligence & The Language of Love, takes an in-depth look at ego. Consider how you define yourself and how to live a happier life, apart from ego in your career, relationships, and health.

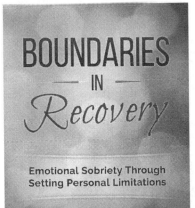

Opiate Addiction